The Coming of God's Kingdom

KAY ARTHUR
PETE De LACY

HARVEST HOUSE PUBLISHERS

EUGENE, OREGON

All Scripture quotations are taken from New American Standard Bible®, © 1960, 1962, 1963, 1968, 1971, 1972, 1973, 1975, 1977, 1995 by The Lockman Foundation. Used by permission. (www.Lockman.org)

Cover by Koechel Peterson & Associates, Inc., Minneapolis, Minnesota

THE COMING OF GOD'S KINGDOM

Copyright © 2009 by Precept Ministries International
Published by Harvest House Publishers
Eugene, Oregon 97402
www.harvesthousepublishers.com

Library of Congress Cataloging-in-Publication Data

Arthur, Kay, 1933-
    The coming of God's kingdom / Kay Arthur and Pete De Lacy.
        p. cm.—(The new inductive study series)
    Includes bibliographical references.
    ISBN 978-0-7369-2512-9 (pbk.)
    Bible. N.T. Matthew—Textbooks. I. De Lacy, Pete. II. Title
    BS2575.55.A78 2009
    226.2'0071—dc22

                                                                    2008032121

Printed in the United States of America

09 10 11 12 13 14 15 16 / BP-NI / 10 9 8 7 6 5 4 3 2 1

CONTENTS

༄ ༄ ༄ ༄

How to Get Started...

∿∿∿∿

Reading directions is sometimes difficult and hardly ever enjoyable! Most often you just want to get started. Only if all else fails will you read the instructions. We understand, but please don't approach this study that way. These brief instructions are a vital part of getting started on the right foot! These few pages will help you immensely.

FIRST

As you study Matthew, you will need four things in addition to this book:

1. A Bible that you are willing to mark in. The marking is essential. An ideal Bible for this purpose is *The New Inductive Study Bible (NISB)*. The *NISB* is in a single-column text format with large, easy-to-read type, which is ideal for marking. The margins of the text are wide and blank for note taking.

The *NISB* also has instructions for studying each book of the Bible, but it does not contain any commentary on the text, nor is it compiled from any theological stance. Its purpose is to teach you how to discern truth for yourself through the inductive method of study. (The map and chart in the appendix of this study guide are taken from the *NISB*.)

Whichever Bible you use, just know you will need to mark in it, which brings us to the second item you will need...

2. A fine-point, four-color ballpoint pen or various colored fine-point pens that you can use to write in your Bible. Office supply stores should have those.

3. Colored pencils or an eight-color leaded Pentel pencil.

4. A composition book or a notebook for working on your assignments and recording your insights.

SECOND

1. As you study Matthew, you will be given specific instructions for each day's study. These should take you between 20 and 30 minutes a day, but if you spend more time than this, you will increase your intimacy with the Word of God and the God of the Word.

If you are doing this study in a class and you find the lessons too heavy, simply do what you can. To do a little is better than to do nothing. Don't be an all-or-nothing person when it comes to Bible study.

Remember, anytime you get into the Word of God, you enter into more intensive warfare with the devil (our enemy). Why? Every piece of the Christian's armor is related to the Word of God. And our one and only offensive weapon is the sword of the Spirit, which is the Word of God. The enemy wants you to have a dull sword. Don't cooperate! You don't have to!

2. As you read each chapter, train yourself to ask the "5 W's and an H": who, what, when, where, why, and how. Asking questions like these helps you see exactly what the Word of God is saying. When you interrogate the text with the 5 W's and an H, you ask questions like these:

a. **What** is the chapter about?

b. **Who** are the main characters?

c. **When** does this event or teaching take place?

d. **Where** does this happen?

e. **Why** is this being done or said?

f. **How** did it happen?

3. Locations are important in many books of the Bible, so marking references to these in a distinguishable way will be helpful to you. I simply underline every reference to a location in green (grass and trees are green!) using my four-color ballpoint pen. A map is included in the appendix of this study so you can look up the locations.

4. References to time are also very important and should be marked in an easily recognizable way in your Bible. I mark them by putting a clock like this 🕐 in the margin of my Bible beside the verse where the phrase occurs. You may want to underline or color the references to time in one specific color.

5. You will be given certain key words to mark throughout this study. This is the purpose of the colored pencils and the colored pens. If you will develop the habit of marking your Bible in this way, you will find it will make a significant difference in the effectiveness of your study and in how much you remember.

A **key word** is an important word that the author uses repeatedly in order to convey his message to his readers. Certain key words will show up throughout Matthew; others will be concentrated in a specific chapter. When you mark a key word, you should also mark its synonyms (words that mean the same thing in the context) and any pronouns (*he, his, she, her, it, we, they, us, our, you, their, them*) in the same way you have marked the key word. Also, mark each word the same way in all of its forms (such as *judge, judgment,* and *judging*). We will give you a few suggestions for ways to mark key words in your daily assignments.

You can use colors or symbols or a combination of colors and symbols to mark words for easy identification. However, colors are easier to distinguish than symbols. When we use symbols, we keep them very simple. For example, you could draw a red heart around the word *love* and shade the inside of the heart like this: love.

When I mark the members of the Godhead (which I do not always mark), I color each word yellow and mark the *Father* with a purple triangle like this: God. I mark the *Son* this way: Jesus Christ and the *Holy Spirit* this way: Spirit.

When marking key words, mark them in a way that is easy for you to remember. Devising a color-coding system for marking key words throughout your Bible will help you instantly see where a key word is used. You might want to make yourself a bookmark listing the words you mark along with their colors and/or symbols.

6. A chart called MATTHEW AT A GLANCE is included in the appendix of this book. As you complete your study of a chapter, record the main theme of that chapter under the appropriate chapter number. The main theme of a chapter is what the chapter deals with the most. It may be a particular subject or teaching.

If you will fill out the MATTHEW AT A GLANCE chart as you progress through the study, you will have a synopsis of Matthew when you are finished. If you have a *New Inductive Study Bible,* you will find the same chart in your Bible (page 1613). If you record your themes there, you will have them for a ready reference.

7. Always begin your study with prayer. As you do your part to handle the Word of God accurately, you must

remember that the Bible is a divinely inspired book. The words that you are reading are truth, given to you by God so you can know Him and His ways more intimately. These truths are divinely revealed.

> For to us God revealed them through the Spirit; for the Spirit searches all things, even the depths of God. For who among men knows the thoughts of a man except the spirit of the man which is in him? Even so the thoughts of God no one knows except the Spirit of God (1 Corinthians 2:10-11).

Therefore ask God to reveal His truth to you as He leads and guides you into all truth. He will if you will ask.

8. Each day when you finish your lesson, meditate on what you saw. Ask your heavenly Father how you should live in light of the truths you have just studied. At times, depending on how God has spoken to you through His Word, you might even want to write LFL ("Lessons for Life") in the margin of your Bible and then, as briefly as possible, record the lesson for life that you want to remember.

THIRD

This study is set up so that you have an assignment for every day of the week—so that you are in the Word daily. If you work through your study in this way, you will find it more profitable than doing a week's study in one sitting. Pacing yourself this way allows time for thinking through what you learn on a daily basis!

The seventh day of each week differs from the other six days. The seventh day is designed to aid group discussion; however, it's also profitable if you are studying this book individually.

The "seventh" day is whatever day in the week you choose to finish your week's study. On this day, you will find a verse or two for you to memorize and Store in Your Heart. Then there is a passage to Read and Discuss. This will help you focus on a major truth or major truths covered in your study that week.

To assist those using the material in a Sunday school class or a group Bible study, there are Questions for Discussion or Individual Study. Even if you are not doing this study with anyone else, answering these questions would be good for you.

If you are in a group, be sure every member of the class, including the teacher, supports his or her answers and insights from the Bible text itself. Then you will be handling the Word of God accurately. As you learn to see what the text says and compare Scripture with Scripture, the Bible explains itself.

Always examine your insights by carefully observing the text to see what it *says*. Then, before you decide what the passage of Scripture *means,* make sure that you interpret it in the light of its context. Scripture will never contradict Scripture. If it ever seems to contradict the rest of the Word of God, you can be certain that something is being taken out of context. If you come to a passage that is difficult to understand, reserve your interpretations for a time when you can study the passage in greater depth.

The purpose of the Thought for the Week is to share with you what we consider to be an important element in your week of study. We have included it for your evaluation and, we hope, for your edification. This section will help you see how to walk in light of what you learned.

Books in the New Inductive Study Series are survey courses. If you want to do a more in-depth study of a particular book of the Bible, we suggest you do a Precept Upon

Precept Bible study course on that book. You may obtain more information on these courses by contacting Precept Ministries International at 800-763-8280, visiting our website at www.precept.org, or filling out and mailing the response card in the back of this book.

INTRODUCTION TO MATTHEW

~~~~

Among the earliest of the 27 books of the New Testament are the four Gospels. Our English word *gospel* is a translation of the Greek word *evaggelion,* which means "good news." The gospel in the New Testament is the good news about Jesus Christ. The Gospel of Matthew is Matthew's account of this good news.

Three of the Gospels—Matthew, Mark, and Luke—are called the Synoptic Gospels, meaning they present a common point of view. However, several characteristics distinguish them. For example, Luke tells us in the opening that his account is "in consecutive order." The other Gospels don't make that claim. Matthew has a unique perspective and purpose we'll let you discover for yourself.

As we study the Gospels, we don't need to cross-reference every teaching and activity to build a "harmony" of the Gospels—a number of authors have done this work for us. In fact, you'll find a concise harmony of the Gospels in the *New Inductive Study Bible* on pages 2117–2122. Such charts show at a glance where a particular teaching or activity occurs in other Gospels or if it is unique to just one. You may find such a harmony helpful at times, but we want to discover Matthew's unique perspective, so we'll stick to studying his Gospel for now. Occasionally we'll refer to the others for specific points that are too delicious to miss!

MATTHEW

THE KING

The last of the books included in the Jewish Scriptures (the Old Testament) was written about 400 years before the events of the New Testament. God sent messengers (prophets) to Israel, warning of His coming judgment on idolatry because of the nation's disobedience. Judgment came as promised. God's prophets also promised deliverance by a descendant of David, one anointed by God to restore His people to their proper relationship to Him. Since the Babylonian exile, David's throne sat empty. Foreign rulers installed men of their choosing to be kings over God's people. Sometimes they even chose high priests. For 400 years, Israel looked for a Messiah to conquer their oppressors and restore the throne of David. When would God fulfill this promise?

DAY ONE

As you read a book of the Bible, try to pick up on the author's emphases. Notice his repeated key words and phrases. To see these better, we'll mark them throughout Matthew. A good technique is to record key words and phrases (and the way you plan to mark them) on a three-by-five index card to use as a bookmark. Doing this will help you mark consistently and save lots of time and frustration.

Read through Matthew 1 without stopping. What are the first 17 verses about? How about verses 18-25?

The first thing to figure out is what the point of the genealogy is and then mark only the key figures that give us that main idea. Reading *all* the names can be tedious, especially if they're hard to pronounce!

So, what's the central idea in verses 1-17? Whose genealogy is it, and what relationships are important? Read the text again and mark *Jesus* and how He is described. Also mark references to time.

Now read through Matthew 1:18-25 again, marking *Jesus,* the *Holy Spirit, angel, God,* and references to time. Mark the word *Son* when it refers to Jesus, and add these words to your bookmark. What event is the main topic of these verses?

As you study, you'll see key phrases that recur in Matthew but appear only once in a passage. We find two examples in these verses. What did the angel do? Read Matthew 1:18-25 again, this time marking the entire phrase *an angel of the Lord appeared to him in a dream.* Underline or highlight it. You'll see it again in chapter 2.

Another key phrase in Matthew is to *fulfill what was spoken by the Lord through the prophet.* The text it refers to is in small capital letters. This is the way the New American Standard Bible designates an Old Testament quote in the New Testament. Mark this phrase in Matthew 1:18-25. What happened that fulfilled the prophecy?

Usually cross-references in the Bible include Old Testament passages as well. If you've studied Isaiah, you may recall the context of this statement and what it was designed to do (see Isaiah 7:14; 8:10).

Now, what did you learn about Jesus in this first chapter? Whose Son is He? In what way is He that person's Son? What names is He given, and what do they mean?

Now determine a theme for this chapter and record it on MATTHEW AT A GLANCE in the appendix.

DAY TWO

Don't forget to begin your study time with prayer. Remember, you have access to the Author, and He truly wants you to know, understand, and live by every word that comes from His mouth.

You've observed the first chapter of this Gospel. Now let's dig a little deeper. What three things did we learn about Jesus in verse 1?

The Hebrew word translated "Messiah" and the Greek word translated "Christ" both mean "anointed one." The NASB translates the Hebrew word as "anointed" in all but two verses in the Old Testament (Daniel 9:25-26) and applies it to several kings. However, the concept of a final Messiah who delivers Israel is established by many passages.

The titles Matthew gives Jesus in the first verse are all important to Jews. Why? Read these verses to learn the importance of the title "Son of David":

2 Samuel 7:8-13,16

2 Chronicles 21:7

Jeremiah 23:5-6

Now read these verses to see the importance of the title "Son of Abraham":

Genesis 12:1-3

Genesis 15:1-6

Galatians 3:16

The history of Israel is often marked by key incidents that become turning points or milestones in the progression of its relationship to God. These milestones include God's call and promises to Abraham, the Exodus, the giving of the Law, the entrance to the promised land, the establishment of kings, the division of the kingdom, and the Assyrian and Babylonian captivities. Often major characters accompany these events, like Abraham, David, and Jesus. Matthew 1 refers to one of these major events: the deportation to Babylon.

In case you aren't familiar with Israel's history following David's monarchy, here's the short version. The 12 tribes of Israel split into two kingdoms after king Solomon, David's son, died. The northern kingdom, called Israel, established its own worship system and priesthood apart from Jerusalem. After several hundred years of prophets calling the children of Israel to repent of their idolatries, God sent them off to captivity. Assyria took the northern tribes captive and settled them in other lands, and they never returned.

The southern kingdom, called Judah, fell into idolatry in spite of its temple and Levitical priesthood in Jerusalem. Even seeing what God did to the northern kingdom didn't help. The Babylonians deported the people to Babylon after destroying Jerusalem and its temple, but a remnant later returned to rebuild both.

From the return of the remnant until Jesus' birth, no king ruled on David's throne, although the Jews kept track of genealogies to determine the lineage of their Messiah-King.

The long version of Israel's history involves studying Kings, Chronicles, Ezra, Nehemiah, and the prophets. After you study these books, you'll be familiar with the names of the kings in Matthew 1:7-11. They are kings of Judah, the southern kingdom, the line from David to the Messiah.

To summarize, why are these titles for Jesus—Messiah, son of David, and son of Abraham—so important?

DAY THREE

Now let's dig deeper into Matthew 1:18-25. The virgin birth is critical to understanding the atonement Jesus accomplished on the cross.

Who are Jesus' mother and father? What role does the Holy Spirit play?

Read Isaiah 7:14. How long was Mary a virgin? Why is her virginity an issue?

Read Romans 5:12 and 6:23. If Jesus were born of a human father, what would He inherit from Adam?

Read the following verses to see why Jesus had to be human without a human father:

> Hebrews 10:4-5
>
> Hebrews 2:9,14-17
>
> John 1:29
>
> Hebrews 10:10-18

Do you understand the critical nature of Jesus' virgin birth? Take a few moments to praise God for His love for us.

DAY FOUR

Read through Matthew 2 without stopping. Just notice the major characters and events.

Who are the major characters? Read the chapter again

and mark *king* (two kings are mentioned). Also mark *child* differently from the way you mark *Jesus*. *Child* is used only in chapter 2, so don't add it to your bookmark.

Mark Scriptures that specify dreams and the fulfillment of prophecy.

Double underline the geographical references you find in green and then check the map in the appendix to see where they are relative to each other.

DAY FIVE

Lots of people have misconceptions about the men visiting from the east. The NASB calls them "magi"; other translations say "wise men." We don't mean to ruin the Christmas stories and carols, but from what you've observed in God's Word, how many were there? How many camels did they have? And were they kings? What color was their skin? How were they dressed? What gifts did they bring?

Now, seriously, what titles did they give to Jesus?

What title did Herod have? What problems did their question stir up?

Was Herod the only one who was troubled? Why would anyone else be troubled by these visitors from the east inquiring about the birth of the King of the Jews, the Messiah?

When Herod asked the chief priests and scribes where the Messiah would be born, what was their answer?

What were Herod's false motive and his true motive for secretly calling the magi to determine the exact time the star appeared?

How did the wise men react to Jesus' birth?

Why did the wise men go home a different way rather than tell Herod what they found?

DAY SIX

Now let's look at Herod's reaction to Jesus' birth and what it caused. What did the angel warn Joseph about? Read Matthew 2:12,16 again very carefully.

Did Herod tell the truth to the wise men (Matthew 2:8)? List how his actions reveal what he believed about Jesus. Why did he include the "vicinity" of Bethlehem (verse 16)? Why male children less than two years of age?

Matthew 2:18 quotes Jeremiah 31:15. Rachel was Jacob's wife, the mother of Joseph and Benjamin. Jeremiah refers to her figuratively, describing mourning for the exiles. Matthew uses these words to describe the mourning after the slaughter of the baby boys in Bethlehem. In both cases, the deep sorrow contrasted sharply with the joy to come.

Consult the chart *Herod's Family Tree* in the appendix. It will help you understand Herod's relationship with Archelaus (both mentioned in Matthew 2) and other family members mentioned in Matthew. You'll note on the chart that historians place the date of Herod's death at 4 BC. The text is clear that Herod was alive when Jesus was born, so our dating system of AD (*anno domini*—Latin for "in the year of our Lord") and BC (before Christ) is off by at least four years. It's a long story, but when the calendar calculations were done in the sixth century, a mistake was made that's never been changed.

As the last two exercises for this week, list what God revealed to Joseph in dreams. Start with Matthew 1. Also list all prophecies fulfilled.

Think on these things, and then record a theme for Matthew 2 on MATTHEW AT A GLANCE.

DAY SEVEN

Store in your heart: Matthew 1:23

Read and discuss: Matthew 1:1,17-25; 2.

QUESTIONS FOR DISCUSSION OR INDIVIDUAL STUDY

- ∾ Discuss what you learned from Jesus' genealogy, especially with respect to the history of Israel. Would Jewish readers consider this important? Why or why not?

- ∾ What do you learn about Jesus from the titles Matthew gives Him in chapter 1?

- ∾ Discuss the fulfillment of prophecy in Matthew 1–2.

- ∾ Discuss the importance of fulfilled Scripture to a Jewish audience. Read Acts 17:1-3 with this in mind.

- ∾ Discuss God's revelations through dreams.

- ∾ Contrast the reactions of the wise and the unwise to the birth of Jesus. What parallel do you see today?

THOUGHT FOR THE WEEK

Jesus was a Jew. I know this is painfully obvious, but sometimes I wonder if Christians forget it. Jesus was born to Jews. He was the Messiah of the Jews. Now, if you want to convince someone of this, what do you have to establish?

Well, first of all, that He's Jewish. So how do you do that? You point to His parents, grandparents, and so on. That is, you give His genealogy. But how do we know this Jesus is the Messiah? What's your evidence? Anyone can claim to be the Messiah, but how can we authoritatively say Jesus is the real one?

First you have to know what had been said about the Messiah. Where do you start? The concept of the Messiah emerged in the Old Testament writings. So to show that Jesus is the Messiah, we need to see what the Old Testament predicted about Him. Then we can then show how Jesus fulfilled these predictions.

In Matthew 1–2 we see events in the birth and early life of Jesus that fulfilled Scripture. When the apostle Paul came to a city, he engaged Jews in synagogues on the Sabbath. His custom was to reason with them from the Scriptures. In Acts 17:1-3, Paul reasoned with Jews in a synagogue for three Sabbaths:

> Now when they had traveled through Amphi-polis and Apollonia, they came to Thessalonica, where there was a synagogue of the Jews. And according to Paul's custom, he went to them, and for three Sabbaths reasoned with them from the Scriptures, explaining and giving evidence that the Christ had to suffer and rise again from the dead, and saying, "This Jesus whom I am proclaiming to you is the Christ."

Like Paul, Matthew uses the Scriptures to show the Jews who Jesus is. He shows how prophecy is fulfilled. In just the first two chapters of Matthew, we've seen the fulfillment of five prophecies.

"Behold, the virgin shall be with child, and shall bear a son, and they shall call His name Immanuel" (Matthew 1:23). This verse alone has elements that are mind-boggling. First, a virgin shall be pregnant. Second, the child will be a son. Third, they will name Him Immanuel. I'll grant that anyone can name a child Immanuel. But can *any* virgin become pregnant and produce a forecasted male?

Imagine telling your friends the Messiah was born. When they ask you how you know, you say, "Well, someone predicted that a virgin would become pregnant without sex and have a son, and it all happened!"

"Not enough proof for me!" they say. "What else you got?"

"Well, the Scriptures say the Messiah would be born in Bethlehem, and He was!"

"Tut, tut," they say, "mere coincidence."

So you add that the Scripture said God would call His Son out of Egypt, and this little boy and His family fled to Egypt to avoid being killed by king Herod. Then when Herod ordered the death of all the little boys two years old and younger in Bethlehem and the vicinity, this fulfilled Scripture too. Finally, when Jesus and His family came home from Egypt, they settled in Nazareth, and that ful-filled another prophecy. "Five prophecies fulfilled! Isn't it awesome? That proves it, right?"

Well, it isn't enough. It wasn't for the Jews then, and it isn't today. If it were enough, the whole world would believe! We're going to see many more fulfilled prophecies in Matthew, and still the people rejected Jesus. Many craved signs—miracles to prove He was the one. Yet even when they saw those miracles, they decided He was doing them with Satan's power, not God's.

Miracles don't create belief. Evidence is not proof. We all know that. We doubt, every one of us. We don't believe just because some silvery-tongued orator presents a great PowerPoint presentation. We can't reason our way to faith; God has to open our eyes. Evidence doesn't get us there; God has to give us facts.

You'll see this when we get to Matthew 16, where Jesus praises Peter for believing truth that God, not man, revealed to him.

If truth were the product of a man-made process, man could patent the design, manufacture it, and distribute it, and the world would have it. But the truth is, spiritual things are spiritually appraised (1 Corinthians 2:14). All the evidence in the world won't convince. Instead, truth must be revealed. That's the beauty and mystery of revelation. God's Word has supernatural power to reveal its Author to us. You'll see this when you study Matthew. Isaiah prophesies an event, and it happens. Yet the people didn't understand. Nor did they understand when Jesus spoke to them or when He performed miracles right before their eyes.

Regardless of how many prophecies God fulfilled, most people still didn't believe.

THE KINGDOM

∾∾∾∾

Every king has a kingdom. If Jesus is king of the Jews, what's His kingdom called? Well, that's where the surprise starts. The kingdom has a different name because it's a different kind of kingdom. What is this kingdom like, what does it include, where is it, who are its subjects, and how long does it last? Let's find out.

DAY ONE

Read Matthew 3 today, marking the key words on your bookmark. Also mark *repent, baptize, kingdom, fire,* and *John the Baptist.* Add these to your bookmark. Also mark references to geography and time. Refer to the map in the appendix for locations.

DAY TWO

List all you learn about John the Baptist. The other Gospels have more to say about his relationship to Jesus, but what we see here in chapter 3 is the most important.

29

As you read the text ask the 5 W's and an H questions, like what was John doing? What was he saying? How did various people respond to his message?

Matthew 3:3 quotes Isaiah 40:3. Read Isaiah 40:1-5. What did you discover in the surrounding verses?

What does God promise in Isaiah 40:1-2? How will this come about, according to verses 3-5?

Now let's examine the content of John the Baptist's preaching, this time asking more 5 W's and an H questions: Who came to hear John? Where were they from? What did John tell them to understand, believe, and do? What warning did he give them?

(Sadducees and Pharisees were leading groups in the Jewish community in the first century. They held different beliefs, and both had followers.)

John's message was "Repent!" What does *repent* mean? Read these verses and summarize what you learn about repentance:

Isaiah 55:6-9

Isaiah 44:21-23

Jeremiah 3:11-15

Deuteronomy 30:1-3

DAY THREE

Let's focus today on the one coming after John the Baptist. How is He different from John the Baptist?

What does "baptize you with...fire" mean (verse 11)? Are there other references to fire in this passage, or is this fire unique?

What happened when Jesus came to be baptized?

What significance do you place on verse 15? What does "fulfill all righteousness" mean?

Now, list exactly what happened when Jesus came up out of the water. Do you see evidence of a triune God? If so, what?

Finally, thinking about all you saw yesterday and today, what's the main subject of this chapter? Record this theme for Matthew 3 on MATTHEW AT A GLANCE in the appendix.

DAY FOUR

Read Matthew 4 and mark the key words on your bookmark, time references, and geographical locations. Mark every reference to the *devil,* including synonyms and pronouns. Add *devil* and *Satan* and references to them like *demons* and *spirits* to your key word bookmark. Some people like to use a red pitchfork.

Mark every reference to *Jesus* in this chapter. Also mark *follow* if it refers to following Jesus, and add it to your key word bookmark.

DAY FIVE

Today's focus is Matthew 4:1-11. What was Satan trying to do in this dialogue? List the temptations and how Jesus responded to each one.

The pinnacle was the highest point of the temple. Some think it was the southeast corner of the temple mount platform on which the temple was built. Others think it was the highest point of the temple building itself.

What do Jesus' responses have in common?

Read Hebrews 4:14-16. Learn all you can about Jesus' temptations and the implications for believers.

DAY SIX

Today's focus is Matthew 4:12-25. First, when did these events occur relative to those in Matthew 3? We'll learn more about John and his imprisonment later in Matthew.

Compare Matthew 4:12-13 with Matthew 2:22-23; then read Isaiah 9:1-2; 60:1-3.

What light dawned on the people in darkness (Matthew 4:16)?

Now, compare John's message in Matthew 3:2 to Jesus' message in Matthew 4:17.

Also read Mark 1:9-15 and Luke 3:2-9,18. How do these accounts compare? What do we learn about the kingdom of heaven? To grasp what the Jews understood about the coming kingdom, read these verses:

1 Samuel 8:6-7

Psalm 47

Daniel 4:24-26

Daniel 7:13-14

Psalm 103:19

Summarize what you've learned about the kingdom from what you've read.

Read Acts 1:1-3. How did Jesus spend the time between His resurrection and ascension?

Read Acts 28:23,31. How does this help you understand the coming kingdom?

Now the last question for the week: What did you learn from marking *followed,* and how does this apply to you?

Finally, determine a theme for Matthew 4 and record it on MATTHEW AT A GLANCE.

DAY SEVEN

 Store in your heart: Matthew 4:19
Read and discuss: Matthew 3–4

QUESTIONS FOR DISCUSSION OR INDIVIDUAL STUDY

- What was John the Baptist's ministry and message?

- Discuss people's various responses to John's message.

- What did John say about the one coming after him?

- How did Jesus and John interact?

- What did you learn about repentance?

- Discuss the participation of the Father and Spirit at Jesus' baptism.

- Discuss Satan's tempting of Jesus in the wilderness. List what each temptation implies, how Jesus responded, and principles you can apply when you're tempted.

- Discuss Jesus' activities after His time in the wilderness.

- What was Jesus' message, and how does it compare to John's?

∾ What did you learn about following Jesus?

∾ What did you learn about the fulfillment of prophecy?

THOUGHT FOR THE WEEK

Matthew doesn't tell us about the conception and birth of John the Baptist and prophecies about his ministry, but Luke does. Zacharias the priest and his wife, Elizabeth, who was also descended from Aaron, were righteous in the sight of God, walking blamelessly in all His commandments and requirements. They were childless (Elizabeth was barren), but God broke into their lives. As Zacharias was performing his priestly duties one day, Gabriel the angel appeared to him, announcing that he and Elizabeth's prayer for a child had been heard.

Gabriel tells Zacharias he will have a son and name him John, that this son will be great in the eyes of God, and that God will fill him with the Holy Spirit while he is in his mother's womb. He will turn many in Israel back to the Lord and "go as forerunner before Him in the spirit and power of Elijah, to turn the hearts of the fathers back to the children, and the disobedient to the attitude of the righteous, so as to make ready a people prepared for the Lord" (Luke 1:17).

This same Gabriel tells the virgin Mary she'll have a child and call Him Jesus, and that He'll be Son of the Most High, ruling the house of Jacob on the throne of David forever—a kingdom with no end.

Luke says Elizabeth and Mary were relatives and that when Gabriel spoke to Mary, Elizabeth was six months pregnant with John. Mary went to see Elizabeth. When Mary greeted Elizabeth, the baby John leaped in her womb, and Elizabeth was filled with the Holy Spirit.

There's another side to this story that bears telling. Zacharias did not believe Gabriel, so God struck him mute. On the eighth day after John was born, Zacharias and Elizabeth were going to have their baby circumcised, and Elizabeth insisted on naming him John. Relatives protested that no one in their family was named John. But then Zacharias wrote on a tablet, "His name is John" (1:63) to everyone's surprise. Then Zacharias could speak, and everyone recognized that the Lord's hand was on John.

Zacharias was filled with the Holy Spirit. He prophesied of the future ministries of John and Jesus—that John would give people advance knowledge of salvation through the forgiveness of sins and that Jesus would be the horn of salvation. John grew and became strong in spirit, living in deserts until he appeared publicly to Israel.

Now, let's reason through this by tying it back to what we studied this week about the interaction between John and Jesus. We can take several principles to heart and apply them to our own lives so we can serve God better.

The first principle has to do with Zacharias and Elizabeth's desire for a child. How did they handle this desire? They prayed, and God answered their prayer, giving them a son—not just any son, but one with a special calling and ministry. We can take *all* our requests to God!

The second principle has to do with faith. When Zacharias heard he was going to have a child, he didn't believe Gabriel and God took away his speech. Zacharias became mute testimony to the power, faithfulness, and incomprehensible wisdom of God until John was circumcised—when God gave him back his speech. We can always believe God will answer our prayers one way or the other.

The third principle we can draw from this story is regarding the empowering of God through His Holy Spirit. Look at the references to the Holy Spirit in this story. Gabriel announces that John will be filled with the Holy Spirit while yet in his mother's womb. Gabriel also informs Mary that the Holy Spirit will come upon her to conceive Jesus. When Mary, pregnant with Jesus, greeted Elizabeth, who was pregnant with John, Elizabeth was filled with the Holy Spirit and prophesied about Jesus. Then when Zacharias finally believed God at John's circumcision eight days after his birth, he was filled with the Holy Spirit and prophesied about both John's and Jesus' ministries. God empowers people with the Holy Spirit according to His plans and purposes to accomplish His will. What happened to Zacharias, Elizabeth, Mary, John, and Jesus did not happen because they believed or didn't, but because God is sovereign. Zacharias was unable to speak for nine months, but that didn't stop God's plans, and in the end Zacharias declared both the power and purpose of God.

In the case of both Elizabeth and Mary conceiving— Elizabeth in her old age like Sarah (Abraham's wife) and Mary as a young virgin—we learn that nothing is impossible with God.

And maybe there's still another principle. Elizabeth, Mary, and Zacharias all gave testimony to the goodness of God.

THE SERMON ON THE MOUNT, PART ONE

࿇࿇࿇

Jesus went about teaching and proclaiming the gospel of the kingdom and healing people afflicted with diseases and sickness. Large crowds followed Him from Galilee, the Decapolis, Jerusalem, Judea, and from beyond the Jordan. On one occasion He sat on a mountain to teach. This extended discourse became known as the Sermon on the Mount.

DAY ONE

We'll spread our study of the Sermon on the Mount (Matthew 5–7) over two weeks. This week we'll tackle only chapter 5—we don't want to rush through this powerful teaching. The New Inductive Study Series books are surveys, but we particularly need to slow down in these chapters to soak it all in.

Begin by reading Matthew 5–7, stopping only to get a feel for the sermon. There's a lot of meat here as you'll see.

Now that you've whet your appetite, let's dig into Matthew 5. Reread Matthew 5, noting key passages. You'll see key repeated words and phrases that show the sections of the chapter. Mark these sections in pencil so you can change your mind after further study if you need to.

That's enough for today. We'll dig in deeper tomorrow.

DAY TWO

Today we'll go deeper into Matthew 5. This is an important text, so we want to observe it carefully. Careful, repeated observation is the key to accurate interpretation and valid application. You've probably observed how important the word *blessed* and the phrase *I say to you* are in this chapter. If you did, you're already picking up on the principle of identifying key repeated words and phrases, a skill you can apply any time you're studying, even if you don't have a booklet like this one.

Read Matthew 5:1-12. Mark the key words from your bookmark. Also mark *blessed* and add it to your bookmark.

Now, make two columns: "Blessed Are…" and "For…" List what you've seen. Are you able to see whom Jesus considered blessed? How does His opinion compare to the world's view of who is blessed?

Read these verses and summarize what they teach about being blessed—who is blessed and what they endure. Are they considered blessed in the world's eyes?

Luke 9:23-25

Philippians 3:7-11

Philippians 4:11-13

Hebrews 11:23-26

2 Corinthians 4:16-18

2 Corinthians 12:9-10

1 Peter 1:3-9

Now ask yourself these questions: Whom does God promise to bless? Why does He bless them? How does He bless them? Then ask yourself, *Am I blessed?*

DAY THREE

After you pray, read Matthew 5:13-16 and mark the key words from your bookmark.

What two subjects are mentioned? These are metaphors—symbols that teach principles. Write down the two metaphors.

Salt of the earth is one phrase you may have heard used about people. Is it a compliment or a disparaging remark? Biblical use will help us understand it. Read these verses:

Exodus 30:35

Leviticus 2:13

Deuteronomy 29:23

Judges 9:45

2 Kings 2:20-21

Job 6:6

Isaiah 30:23-24

Mark 9:49-50

Colossians 4:5-6

What purposes does salt have? Are some good and some bad? Which use fits the context of Matthew 5:13: preserve, season, purify, or destroy?

Now let's look at *light of the world*. This one's easier! Look up these verses and record what you learn about light:

Psalm 119:105

John 1:4-9

1 John 1:5-7

Ephesians 5:6-14

What do these verses teach us about Christian responsibility?

DAY FOUR

Now read Matthew 5:17-20 and mark the key words on your bookmark. Add *for I say to (tell) you* and any variants that include other words like *truly* or *but*. Mark the phrases the same way.

How did Jesus describe His relationship to the Law? Does this shock you? We hear so much contrast between Law and grace, Old Testament and New…and now He says this? How do we understand this?

It's important to understand Jesus' relationship to the Law, and this is one of the key passages. The other two are Galatians 3 and Romans 3:27–4:25. Read all of these and note the contrast between the Law and faith. That's the context for understanding Jesus' teachings about the Law in the Sermon on the Mount.

DAY FIVE

Jesus moves into another section of His sermon in verse 21. Read Matthew 5:21-37 and mark the key words on your bookmark. In addition to *but I say to you*, you'll see another key repeated phrase: *you have heard*. Mark them both; they frame the rest of the chapter.

Now make two more columns: "You Have Heard" and "But I Say." List the topics Jesus teaches about.

What is Jesus doing? Is this new information? Amplified old information? How do these relate to the idea in verses 17-20 that He will not abolish the Law, but fulfill it?

DAY SIX

We'll finish up Matthew 5 today. Read and mark Matthew 5:38-48. Then add to the two columns you started yesterday from verses 21-37.

Now, comparing with verses 21-37, does Jesus say anything different about these last topics? Let me give you a hint. In verses 21-37, what did Jesus do with what they had heard—clarify and amplify old laws or give new ones? What did He do in verses 38-48?

Read these verses and note what you learn:

Proverbs 20:22; 24:29

Romans 12:14-21

1 Corinthians 4:9-13,16

1 Peter 3:8-17

Now, look for a pattern in chapters 1–5. In chapters 1–2, we're introduced to the King of the Jews. In chapters 3–4, we're introduced to the Kingdom of heaven and the King's authority over disease and sickness. Now, what are we introduced to here in chapter 5? Relate your answer to the King and His kingdom.

Concluding, what's a good theme for Matthew 5? Take

it from the text, looking at key repeated things that were said. Record it on MATTHEW AT A GLANCE.

DAY SEVEN

 Store in your heart: Matthew 5:16
Read and discuss: Matthew 5

QUESTIONS FOR DISCUSSION OR INDIVIDUAL STUDY

∞ Discuss what you observed about who is blessed, how, and why. Draw out applications. How do these truths affect your day-to-day life?

∞ How can you be the salt of the earth?

∞ What does it mean to be a light of the world?

∞ Discuss the relationship of the Law to grace and faith.

∞ Discuss the "You have heard...but I say" topics and what they mean to your life.

∞ What is your greatest challenge from this chapter?

THOUGHT FOR THE WEEK

One of the most challenging ideas in the Sermon on the Mount is Jesus' statement that He did not come to abolish the Law but to fulfill it. We asked you to read parts of Galatians and Romans this week to understand the believer's relationship to the Law with respect to salvation. This is as controversial today as it was in New Testament times. Back then, a sect of Jews believed in Jesus but taught that you had to keep ritual laws like circumcision to be saved. They were called Judaizers. This controversy arose because Gentiles were coming to faith, and some Jewish believers insisted that they had to be circumcised.

As situations arose, God revealed more truth to His servants, which they recorded in books after these Gospels. This later revelation explains what was said earlier (this is called *progressive revelation*).

The book of Acts records how the elders in Jerusalem settled the matter of circumcision: Gentiles' hearts are cleansed by faith, not by works of the Law. The elders required Gentile believers to abstain from eating meat dedicated to idols, eating blood, and fornicating. The Bible teaches about these things, but we'll pass over them to concentrate on what applies to our study of the Sermon on the Mount and what Jesus meant by fulfilling the Law. The Law prohibited eating certain foods, but Jesus revealed that no food was unclean.

Later, Paul wrote to believers in Galatia because Judaizers were at work there too. He related his previous experiences, forcibly making his point by asking rhetorical questions that exposed error. "Did you receive the Spirit by works of the Law, or by hearing with faith?" (Galatians 3:2).

Ask yourself, "Having begun by the Spirit, are you now being perfected by the flesh [works of the Law]?" (verse 3). The answer, of course, is that if you are justified (declared righteous) by faith, your growth as a Christian happens by faith as well. The righteous person *lives* by faith—he is declared righteous by faith, and he grows in maturity toward greater Christlikeness by faith. The one who trusts in the Law dies by the Law because all those who fail in even one part of it are under a curse. We *live* by faith.

Now, what Galatians 3 makes so very clear is this: God's covenant with Abraham was not invalidated by the covenant

He made with Israel at Mount Sinai (the Law). The Law was added because of sin. It was established to define sin. That's why the smallest stroke of the Law is not done away with. Sin is still sin. But Jesus fulfilled the Law in redeeming us from the Law's curse—the curse of being unable to perform it perfectly.

So the Law is a tutor, a schoolmaster, to lead us to Christ (Galatians 3:23-25). It shows us our sin, our inability to keep the Law perfectly. We need a Savior from both sin and its consequence: death.

Now that faith has come, we're no longer under the tutor, Paul says. The Law has no jurisdiction over those who have come to Christ in faith. It hasn't been abolished, just fulfilled.

THE SERMON ON THE MOUNT, PART TWO

Jesus continues His sermon in chapters 6–7, adding new topics and building on principles established in chapter 5. What new treasures await as we plumb the depths of these timeless truths, learning how we can live in a manner pleasing to God?

DAY ONE

We'll take three days each to cover Matthew 6 and 7. Begin by reading Matthew 6:1-15, marking the key words from your bookmark. Note in the margins of your Bible the topics that are covered. Mark *reward,* but don't add it to your bookmark.

What did you learn about giving in verses 2-4?

What did you learn about prayer in verses 5-8?

What did you learn from marking *reward?* What common principles are given in these two paragraphs?

DAY TWO

Read and mark verses 9-15. Do you recognize this? People often recite this prayer, but another way to look at it is found in Luke 11:1-4, where Jesus' disciples asked Him to teach them how to pray the way John taught his disciples. Note in Matthew 6:9 that Jesus says, "Pray...this way."

If we look to this prayer for a pattern, we can learn a new dimension of prayer. Some categorize the sentences under general headings like worship, allegiance, submission, requests or petition for provisions, confession, and deliverance. Match up each part of the prayers with one of these headings.

What do you think? Can you craft an original prayer using these general headings? Our prayers don't have to contain all these elements. Do you see a principle at the start and finish? What do you see before any requests are made?

If you'd like to study prayer in more depth, try *Lord, Teach Me to Pray in 28 Days*, also published by Harvest House.

DAY THREE

Read and mark Matthew 6:16-34. Mark *treasure* and *worry*[1] and add them to your bookmark.

Another subject like giving and prayer appears. What is it? What are the principles here, and how do they match what you learned in verses 1-7 about giving, prayer, and reward?

What did you learn about treasure in verses 19-24?

What did you learn about worry in verses 25-34?

Now determine a theme for Matthew 6 and record it on MATTHEW AT A GLANCE.

DAYS FOUR & FIVE

Read Matthew 7:1-12 and mark the key words on your bookmark.

Matthew 7:1 is cited like John 3:16 (a lot!). You usually hear it from people who did something they know violates God's Word. It's the knee-jerk reaction of the guilty.

But what is the rest of the passage about? What's the context of that verse? What do you learn about specks and logs in the eye? Does this passage really tell us not to judge? The Greek word translated "judge" means "to distinguish and make a decision."

Read the following for further understanding:

> John 7:24
>
> Romans 2:1-3
>
> James 2:13

Compare Matthew 6:14-15 to Matthew 7:1-5. How do these passages relate to each other?

How does Matthew 7:12 support Matthew 7:1? How does Matthew 7:6 relate to judging?

What have you learned from this text that will help you not be self-righteous and convey a "holier than thou" attitude to the watching world?

Finally, Beloved, what is God's lesson for us? What can we apply to our lives?

DAY SIX

Read Matthew 7:13-29 and mark the key words on your bookmark. List everything you learn about good and bad. Take time to evaluate what you learn about each type of person.

What warning is given in verse 15? How are we taught to differentiate between good and evil in chapter 7?

Now read Matthew 7:13-29 again and mark each word that describes an action. List the references and what Jesus teaches about doing. (Hint: look for synonyms for *acts* like *does* or *puts into practice* in verse 24.)

Record a theme for Matthew 7 on MATTHEW AT A GLANCE.

DAY SEVEN

Store in your heart: Matthew 7:7
Read and discuss: Matthew 6–7

Questions for Discussion or Personal Study

- Discuss what you learned about giving, praying and fasting, and rewards.

- Review the Lord's Prayer and how it can serve as a model for prayer. What principles are involved?

- What does it mean to store up treasures in heaven or on earth?

- Discuss the tension between serving two masters.

- What does Matthew 6 teach about worry? How can you apply this to your life?

- What does "seek first the kingdom of God and His righteousness" mean? How can you do this?

- What did you learn about judging? How does it relate to the Lord's Prayer?

- Discuss the contrast between the good and bad, and fruit. How does this relate to anything you learned in chapter 3?

THOUGHT FOR THE WEEK

As Jesus teaches the crowds on the mountain, He tells them not to be like the hypocrites. If there's one charge the world levels against Christians, it's hypocrisy. They hear what we preach and see the way we live, and when the two don't match up, they cry, "Hypocrite!"

Authentic righteous living is rewarded by God in heaven. The hypocrite gets his full reward from men. That's it for him—forever!

The English word *hypocrite* comes from the Greek word *hupokrisis,* which was used of actors in stage plays who pretend to be others. The idea is clear: The hypocrite isn't what he pretends to be; he's just playing a role.

Those who pretend they are Christians but really aren't give a false impression. True Christians who behave badly also give a false impression.

The distressing thing about this is that both damage the cause of Christ—the kingdom of God is hindered, and the name of Christ is blasphemed.

What can we do? How can we change perceptions and real consequences?

We can't always change people's opinions, but we can act in ways that are consistent with the faith we profess. If we live authentic Christian lives, people will see real Christianity. Some call it "walking the talk." How do we learn to do this? Where is the instruction manual? And where is the power to do this?

Paul's letter to the Ephesians gives us answers to these questions. First, we learn our position in Christ. We are seated with Him at the right hand of the Father in the heavenlies. Although we walk this earth, our true position is in Jesus. We are authentic Christians; Jesus can see it and God can see it, even if people on this earth don't.

We are sealed with the Holy Spirit for the day of redemption. We have the Holy Spirit in us, empowering us to live righteously as authentic Christians. So we have position and power to live in a manner that will keep people from calling us hypocrites.

We're told in Ephesians to stand in faith, to understand our position, to take authority to live authentic Christian lives, and to walk in a manner worthy of our calling. The manner is spelled out; humility leads the list, then gentleness, patience, and tolerance for one another in love. We're instructed to diligently preserve the unity of the Spirit in the bond of peace. Christians fighting other Christians is not preserving the unity of the Spirit in the bond of peace.

We're not to be children tossed about by waves and carried about by every wind of doctrine and the trickery of men, by craftiness in deceitful scheming. We're to know the Bible, the Word of God, and live by it.

We're to put off the old self, all bitterness, wrath, anger, clamor, slander, and malice, and put on the new. We're to be kind to one another, tenderhearted, forgiving each other, just as God in Christ also has forgiven us. Wow! Doesn't this sound like the Sermon on the Mount? Doesn't this sound like the Lord's Prayer?

We're to walk as children of light. We are the light of the world, so we walk in wisdom, not as unwise men but as wise. "Do not get drunk with wine, for that is dissipation, but be filled with the Spirit, speaking to one another in psalms and hymns and spiritual songs, singing and making melody with your heart to the Lord" (Ephesians 5:18-19).

Salt of the earth and light of the world, trusting in God, seeking His kingdom and righteousness. The world will see and know what authentic Christians are, and only those who aren't really Christians will be called hypocrites.

WHAT KIND OF MAN IS THIS?

What kind of man teaches like this? What kind of man heals like this? What kind of man has authority over nature and demons like this? What kind of man *is this*?

DAY ONE

After prayer, read Matthew 8, marking the key words on your bookmark. Add *Son of Man, authority,* and *faith (believe)* to your bookmark. Jesus' titles, like *Son of Man,* are important. When you come to one of these titles, note who uses it.

DAY TWO

Read Matthew 8 again today, noting events that occur. Ask the 5 W's and an H questions: Who were healed? What were they healed from? How did Jesus do the healing?

What does Matthew 8:10-12 imply about the kingdom of heaven? Who asked for healing?

What's significant about Matthew 8:17? Read Isaiah 53:4. (If you have time, read all of Isaiah 53.)

What did the demons ask Jesus? What title did they give Him? (Mark this title in a unique way and look for it throughout Matthew.)

What does the people's response to Jesus casting out demons tell you about them?

Record a theme for Matthew 8 on MATTHEW AT A GLANCE.

DAY THREE

Read Matthew 9, marking key words from your bookmark. Add *sin(s) (sinners)*.

DAY FOUR

As you did in Matthew 8, note events. If people are healed, note who they are, what they were healed of, and how Jesus healed them.

What's significant about Jesus' response to the paralytic? Who challenged Jesus? How did Jesus demonstrate His authority?

Read Matthew 9:14-17 again. What was Jesus really talking about—wine, garments, or something else? Why?

What do you learn about healing and faith in this chapter?

List the various responses to what Jesus did. Who believed? How did the religious authorities respond?

Record a theme for chapter 9 and add it to MATTHEW AT A GLANCE.

DAY FIVE

Read Matthew 9:36–10:42, marking the key words on your bookmark. Chapter breaks are man-made, so we're free to consider others. Do you think it's a good idea to start at Matthew 9:36? How does chapter 10 differ from Matthew 8–9?

DAY SIX

To whom did Jesus send His 12 disciples? What did He commission them to do? How were they to go? What responses did Jesus tell them to expect?

What is the normal response to someone who follows Jesus and does what Jesus commands?

Review the teaching in Matthew 8–9 regarding following Jesus.

Have you experienced any of these things? How does this challenge compare to what many teach about Christian life today?

Finally, determine a theme for Matthew 10 and record it on MATTHEW AT A GLANCE.

DAY SEVEN

Store in your heart: Matthew 8:27
Read and discuss: Matthew 8–10

Questions for Discussion or Individual Study

- ∞ Discuss your insights into the authority Jesus and His disciples demonstrated.

- ∞ Review the various reactions of people to what they saw and heard.

- ∞ What kind of response can a follower of Jesus expect?

- ∞ What's significant about Jesus' encounter with the centurion? What implication is there for non-Jews?

- ∞ How does Jesus' healing ministry relate to forgiveness of sins?

- ∞ How does Jesus and His disciples' healing ministry relate to the kingdom of heaven?

Thought for the Week

What kind of man is this? He cleansed a leper, healed the paralyzed servant of a centurion, cured Peter's mother-in-law's fever with a touch, cast out spirits (demons) with a word, calmed a stormy sea, stopped the winds, cast demons out of men and into swine, healed a paralytic and forgave his sins, healed a woman who had a hemorrhage for 12 years, raised a synagogue official's daughter from the dead, and gave sight to the blind.

He gave authority to His 12 disciples to heal people with every kind of disease and every kind of sickness, and He commissioned them to raise the dead, cleanse the lepers, cast out demons, and preach the presence of the kingdom of God.

What kind of man does these things?

Matthew has given us several descriptions of Jesus. He called Him Messiah, son of David, and son of Abraham in chapter 1. These titles establish that He was the expected one. He had the right credentials. In the same chapter we see that He will be called Jesus because He will save His people from their sins and Immanuel because He is God with us.

In chapter 2 He's called the King of the Jews, and in chapter 3 at His baptism the Father declares from heaven that Jesus is His beloved Son in whom He is well-pleased. The devil recognized that Jesus was the Son of God when he tempted Him in the wilderness.

Crowds were amazed at His sermon on the mountain because He taught with authority, not as their scribes.

The demons He cast out in the land of the Gadarenes knew He was the Son of God. When He healed the paralytic, the crowd was awestruck and glorified God, who had given such authority to men.

What do we learn from these observations? Joseph was told that Jesus would save His people from their sins, but he may not have known that Jesus was the Son of God. John the Baptist saw the Spirit of God descend on Jesus as a dove and heard the voice of God from the heavens.

Satan and his demons recognized Jesus as the Son of God, but the crowds saw Him only as a man empowered by God. Why didn't the people see what Satan and the demons did?

Listen to what God prophesied through Isaiah:

> He said, "Go, and tell this people:
> 'Keep on listening, but do not perceive;
> Keep on looking, but do not understand.'
> "Render the hearts of this people insensitive,
> Their ears dull,

And their eyes dim,
Otherwise they might see with their eyes,
Hear with their ears,
Understand with their hearts,
And return and be healed" (Isaiah 6:9-10).

You'll see this quotation next week, in chapter 13, but it's appropriate here too. Now do you know why the people didn't see what Satan and his demons saw?

The answer is in Jesus' purpose as Messiah. He came for His lost sheep of the house of Israel, "His people." He came to save *them* from their sins. And Jesus came to save Gentiles as well, as we saw when He healed the centurion's servant. Many will recline with Abraham, Isaac, and Jacob in the kingdom of heaven, but many from Israel, the sons of the kingdom, will not be there. Why? Because they don't believe; God has hardened their hearts as Isaiah prophesied.

Satan and his demons made their choice long before Eden was created. They chose to rebel against God, and their future is certain punishment in the lake of fire. They have no chance for redemption. They are not made in God's image. And after man believed Satan's lie, God promised a human seed that would crush the serpent's head, a seed that would redeem mankind.

And now Jesus, the Redeemer, the promised seed, has come. Abraham believed in the seed God promised and was declared righteous. The Son of Abraham has come. Who will believe and be saved? Who will know who He is yet reject Him, fail to worship Him, fail to believe in Him?

What about you? The point of the gospel is to declare the truth about Jesus so people can believe and be saved. That's what sharing the gospel means: witnessing to the lost. The Gospel of Matthew contains that message, but not all who hear will believe. What about *you*? If you have believed, rejoice. But what will you do with this Gospel? Will you study Matthew and just be content, or will you share its message with others, with those who are lost and perishing?

If you haven't believed, will you? Or will you understand the truth about Jesus and yet reject Him as God with us, the Savior, the Son of God who has authority to forgive your sins? What will you do?

CAN YOU DO THE RIGHT THING AND STILL BE HATED?

Have you ever tried as hard as you could to do the right thing, only to discover that a lot of people were angry with you for doing it? Well, you are in good company.

DAY ONE

Read Matthew 11 today, marking the words and phrases on your bookmark. Also mark *generation* and *judgment*. Add these to your bookmark.

DAY TWO

Back in Matthew 3, you began a list on John the Baptist. Add what you learn from Matthew 11 to that list. Now, what did John ask Jesus, and how did Jesus respond?

What miracles do you suppose John had heard about? What kinds of things had Jesus done?

What was John's core message according to Matthew 3? Compare Luke 3:15-17.

List some prophecies in these verses about the coming Messiah:

> Isaiah 35:3-6
>
> Isaiah 61:1-2
>
> Malachi 3:1-3

What does the time reference in Matthew 11:13 tell you?

How is John the Baptist described in verse 14? Compare to Malachi 4:5. Whom did John prepare the way for?

What has John said about a kingdom? Who established the kingdom? Read Luke 22:14-20 and watch for the word *covenant*.

Compare John's message in Matthew 3:1-2 with Jesus' message in Matthew 4:12-17. When did Jesus start preaching this message?

Did anyone oppose the message of the kingdom of heaven? Where was John? Why was he there? Read Luke 3:15-20.

What did you learn from marking *generation* in Matthew 11:16-19?

What cities did Jesus condemn? Why did He single them out? How does this apply to you? Are you accountable for what you know about Jesus?

What do you learn about Jesus and God from Jesus' prayer in Matthew 11:25-27?

Record a theme for Mathew 11 on MATTHEW AT A GLANCE.

DAY THREE

After beginning in prayer, read Matthew 12, marking the key words and phrases from your bookmark. Remember to mark *generation* and *judgment* as you did in Matthew 11.

Record a theme for Matthew 12 on MATTHEW AT A GLANCE.

DAY FOUR

Read Exodus 20:8-11 to see the basic command concerning the Sabbath.

Circumcision, dietary laws, and keeping the Sabbath were the three most important rituals of Judaism. To keep people from breaking the Ten Commandments and purportedly to clarify them, the Pharisees developed an additional system of rules. But often they went beyond God's original intent. Picking grain for your meal and healing, for example, were two of thirty-nine types of work forbidden on the Sabbath.

How does Jesus respond to the Pharisees' challenge in Matthew 12?

Read and compare Luke 6:1-5 and Mark 2:23-28. What does Mark add?

Also read Hosea 6:6, which Jesus uses in His defense.

DAY FIVE

The battle over Sabbath-keeping continues in Matthew. What did the Pharisees ask Jesus in the synagogue? How did He respond this time?

Mark 3:1-6 is a synoptic text (parallel). How did the Pharisees respond?

Now go back and read Matthew 11:28-30. How does Jesus' yoke compare to the Pharisees'?

Matthew tells us Jesus' withdrawal following this confrontation fulfills another prophecy from Isaiah. Compare Matthew 12:15-21 with Isaiah 42:1-4.

What quality did Jesus have that the Pharisees lacked?

DAY SIX

Compare Matthew 12:22-24 to Matthew 9:32-38. What similarities and differences do you see?

How does Jesus respond to the charge of partnering with Satan?

What do you learn about the Holy Spirit in verses 28-32?

Read John 1:29 and 1 John 1:8–2:2. Scripture does not contradict Scripture, so if believers' sins are forgiven, what can you conclude about the sin against the Holy Spirit?

Compare verses 33-37 with Matthew 3:7-10.

What did you learn about "this generation"? Contrast these people with the ones in Jesus' family.

DAY SEVEN

 Store in your heart: Matthew 11:28
Read and discuss: Matthew 11–12

QUESTIONS FOR DISCUSSION OR PERSONAL STUDY

- Discuss John the Baptist's relationship to Jesus and the kingdom of heaven.

- Why did Jesus single out cities for woes?

    ∾ What was the issue with the Sabbath? Describe Jesus'
        yoke and how it contrasts with the Pharisees.'

    ∾ What Old Testament prophecies do you see fulfilled
        in this chapter? Why are these important?

    ∾ Discuss what you learned about the forgiveness of
        sins.

    ∾ Compare how various people in these chapters
        reacted to Jesus' words and actions.

    ∾ How would you have reacted to Jesus? Do you iden-
        tify with the Pharisees and others in Jesus' genera-
        tion?

THOUGHT FOR THE WEEK

When God made a covenant with Abraham, He insti-
tuted circumcision as a sign to show who was in covenant
with Him. In other words, when Abraham and his descen-
dants circumcised their male children, they permanently
and outwardly declared they were in the covenant of the
promised seed. Circumcision of the male reproductive
organ signaled the coming seed who will become a great
nation and in whom all the families of the earth will be
blessed. His kingdom will have no end.

At Mount Sinai, God made a covenant with Israel. We're
familiar with the Ten Commandments, but God revealed
613 commandments that further developed or explained
the original 10. Most of those commandments (365) were
positive, and the rest (248) were negative. Jews claim the
365 correspond to the days of the year and the 248 correspond to the number of bones in man's body.

No one could keep all these laws. But the fourth one,
the command to keep the Sabbath holy, particularly became

a sign that God was the one who sanctifies His covenant people:

> But as for you, speak to the sons of Israel, saying, "You shall surely observe My sabbaths; for this is a sign between Me and you throughout your generations, that you may know that I am the LORD who sanctifies you" (Exodus 31:13).

> Also I gave them My sabbaths to be a sign between Me and them, that they might know that I am the LORD who sanctifies them (Ezekiel 20:12).

> Sanctify My sabbaths; and they shall be a sign between Me and you, that you may know that I am the LORD your God (Ezekiel 20:20).

No other nation in history was explicitly told to "take Saturday off"; in fact, heathen cultures would sooner generate wealth, especially making use of their slaves. But to the Jew, keeping the Sabbath was a holy action. Now here comes Jesus, breaking not the Sabbath but *traditions about* keeping the Sabbath. The fourth commandment says to "remember the sabbath day, to keep it holy." But how do you keep it holy? The rabbis had specified 39 prohibitions, such as not carrying money, walking more than a certain distance (called "a Sabbath-day's journey"), picking grain, carrying loads, lighting fires, cooking, or conducting business. Refrain from these, the rabbis taught, and you are keeping the Sabbath holy.

But as He did in His teaching in the Sermon on the Mount, Jesus explained God's original intent. The Sabbath, He said, was made for man, to give rest from labor, just as God rested from His labor of creation. Man simply needed to stop his regular business and rest. Rescuing animals, healing sick people, or picking up grain to eat did not profane the Sabbath.

Gentiles are not required to perform the Law's rituals, such as circumcision; Paul's explanations in Romans and Galatians make that clear. God commanded circumcision and Sabbath-keeping to Abraham and his seed, Israel.

These rituals no longer define a true relationship to God. We're part of the New Covenant, which gives two other signs to show our relationship to God. The first, baptism, is very much like circumcision in that it is a one-time act. Circumcision was done soon after birth—the eighth day of a male child's life.

Baptism is done soon after the new birth. There's no specific day, but it too is a once-in-a-lifetime act, an outward sign of our commitment to Christ that the community of believers witnesses. Believers' baptism is an outer revelation of inner realities: dying to the old self, rising to new life, identifying with the death and resurrection of Jesus Christ.

The sign that we are in continuing relationship with Christ is the Lord's Supper. We celebrate this meal periodically, just as the Jews continually keep the Sabbath. But the New Covenant does not require the Lord's supper weekly. Baptism and the Lord's supper, then, respectively correspond to the one experience of circumcision and the ongoing keeping of the Sabbath.

The evil and adulterous generation of Jesus' day craved signs. He gave them only Jonah's three-day incarceration and release from the belly of the fish to signify His own death, burial, and resurrection—exactly what we proclaim in both baptism and the Lord's supper. The difference is that the Jews wanted Jesus to prove He was the Messiah, the Son of God, *immediately*—they wanted Him to display miracles long before His death.

WHY DID JESUS SPEAK IN PARABLES?

∾∿∾∿

What is a parable? Why did Jesus recite them to all who would listen, but then explain them only to His followers (Mark 4:11)?

DAYS ONE & TWO

We're going to spend the entire week on Matthew 13 because it's so rich. You'll start by observing Matthew 13 today and tomorrow, marking the words on your bookmark. Remember to keep interrogating the text with *who*, *what*, *when*, *where*, *why*, and *how* questions. Mark *parable*, *heaven*, *seed(s)*, *hear*, and *understand*. You'll see *of heaven* connected to *kingdom*, which is already on your bookmark, but mark it differently.

DAY THREE

Now go back through the chapter and mark each of the parables with a pencil. Put a line at the beginning and the end of each. The goal of this exercise is simply to see where the parables are.

Now number them and specify the main subject with a word like *sower* or *tares*.

The word *parable* comes from two Greek words meaning "to throw alongside." The main idea is to illustrate or explain something unknown by comparing it with something known, something "thrown alongside," so to speak. Find the article in the appendix titled "Interpreting and Understanding Parables." Study these principles.

Now according to Matthew 13:10-17, why did Jesus use parables? Read Isaiah 1:1-4,10-20 and Isaiah 6 to understand how Jesus' parables fulfill Isaiah's prophecy.

According to Matthew 12:22-37, what is the spiritual condition of the Pharisees?

DAY FOUR

Now let's dig into the parables. The first, the parable of the sower in verses 3-9, specifies four places where seeds fall and four respective results (some yield nothing). Verses 18-23 tell us what the seed and the soils represent. In one sentence, what is this parable about?

How do the four soils fit the two kinds of listeners Jesus has mentioned so far in Matthew? Read Matthew 7:15-19,24-27; 10:32-33. How would a farmer interpret the soils in terms of obedient or disobedient listening?

What does this parable teach about bearing fruit? Read Matthew 3:1-10, Luke 6:43-45, and John 15:1-8. What are the relationships between fruit, the heart, and abiding in Jesus?

Think about what you learned. What can you apply?

Friend, what is the Lord showing you? Are you completely

sold out to Him? What is the seed He has sown in your heart producing? Before you finish your study time today, spend time in prayer, seeking His face. Ask Him to show whether you lack any fruit. Cry out to Him; He will hear; He will respond; He will heal.

DAY FIVE

Parables have one *main* point—just one. Be careful not to mistake a detail for the main point. Generally, details set up the story, but we should focus our attention on the main point. On the other hand, Jesus sometimes gives meaning to details, so here is a way to maintain balance: Let Him give meaning to details; if He doesn't, we shouldn't.

Now let's look at the second parable—the wheat and tares (weeds). Read Matthew 13:24-58 and mark *wheat* as you did *seed* on day 1. Mark comparisons, which are often introduced with the words *like* or *as*.

Note what all the symbols represent: the field, the sowers, the good and bad seeds, the tares (weeds that looks like wheat until the harvest), and the harvest.

When does the harvest take place? What's the main point of the parable?

DAY SIX

List the main point of each of the remaining parables in a few words.

What's the parable in verses 47-50 about? What is the kingdom of heaven compared to? How is its message similar to the main point of the parable of the tares?

What is the kingdom of heaven compared to in the two parables in verses 31-33? What contrast does the word *but* in verse 32 introduce us to?

How do the growths of the little leaven and little mustard compare?

Two more short parables are in verses 44-46. In each, the kingdom of heaven is compared to something. Note what it is and what value the parable places on it. How valuable is the kingdom of heaven to you?

In verse 51, Jesus asks His disciples if they understand the parables. Would you answer the same way they did?

Record a theme for Matthew 13 on MATTHEW AT A GLANCE.

DAY SEVEN

 Store in your heart: Matthew 13:44

Read and discuss: Matthew 13

QUESTIONS FOR DISCUSSION OR INDIVIDUAL STUDY

- ❧ Discuss Jesus' purposes for teaching in parables.

- ❧ How do these parables relate to Isaiah's prophecy?

- ❧ Discuss each of the parables in this chapter. For each, identify what the kingdom of heaven is compared to and other details Jesus explains. Then write out the main point of each.

- ❧ What applications can you make? How do you relate to each parable? How do you relate to Matthew 13:16?

Thought for the Week

When Jesus taught in parables, He drew from familiar surroundings. For example, with respect to the parable of the sower, the types of soils were all around. The countryside around the Sea of Galilee is rocky, the result of volcanic activity that littered the area with black basalt rocks. One of the more common plants was the thistle (today as well), a thorny plant that chokes out crops.

In wheat fields today in Israel it's common to see tares, weeds that look like wheat until the grain is ready for harvest. Fishing with nets was normal on the Sea of Galilee, though today the lake is more commonly used for recreation.

So Jesus illustrated the kingdom of heaven with familiar things in His surroundings. But He revealed the meaning of the kingdom only to His disciples (Matthew 13:11).

God told Isaiah that Israel would keep on listening but not perceive, keep on looking but not understand. He also said someone was coming who would open blind eyes. The prophecies of the Messiah in the Old Testament and their fulfillment in the Gospel of Matthew clearly show that Jesus is the Messiah. Only those who are blind, who cannot hear, who live in darkness, reject this truth.

So Jesus spoke in parables. He used imagery everyone could understand but granted the meanings only to His followers. Even though He performed miracles, the blind in heart could not see. They could not because they were not given eyes to see. As Isaiah said, "He has blinded their eyes and He hardened their heart; so that they would not see with their eyes and perceive with their heart, and be converted and I heal them" (John 12:40).

So it is today. Only those who humble themselves to receive God's Word can see with the heart. God speaks to us in clear language we can understand. He uses ideas easy for the common person to understand, but we need eyes to see and ears to hear.

Because God speaks ordinary language (not special, heavenly, or obscure words), every person can understand the gospel.

Paul's letter to the Romans tells us that God made Himself known in creation, so all people are without excuse. God speaks a universal language. Creation shows us His power, wisdom, provision, magnificence, transcendence, and holiness. It shows us we're not God. When we compare ourselves to the Creator, we see that we're much less and, by comparison, in need of someone to lift us up. And God does that Himself. He purchases us from slavery to sin by shedding the precious blood of His Son, Jesus, the Messiah.

It's really so simple, many can't believe it. They think it has to be complicated, expensive, or difficult. But it's not. Jesus used parables to keep the blind from seeing the truth. God is holy; we are sinners by inheritance from Adam. Sin separates us from God, and the only remedy is the sacrifice of a sinless man not descended by blood from Adam. Jesus was that man. All God asks us to do is believe this truth: Our reconciliation to Him through Jesus' death for our sins is a matter of faith, not works, not money, not talent, not anything based on us…just (and all) on Him.

That's why the questions this week asked you about seeing yourself in these parables. What are you? Wheat or tare? Good soil or rocky? What do you believe?

WHAT KIND OF FAITH DO YOU HAVE?

∾∾∾∾

What kind of faith do you have? Great faith? Little faith? No faith? What did Jesus say about these different kinds of faith, and what does it matter to you or me?

DAY ONE

Read Matthew 14, marking key words from your book-mark. Add *compassion* and *worship*. Don't forget to mark time and geographical references.

DAYS TWO & THREE

Now read Matthew 14 again and note or mark with a pencil in your Bible where each event is occurring. You may want to note this in the margins.

Now let's look at these events individually. Who are the main characters, and what happens in verses 1-12? (A tetrarchy is rule by four, so a tetrarch is one of four rulers in a land.) The chart HEROD'S FAMILY TREE in the appendix will help you sort out relationships between the people mentioned.

Read Luke 3:1-3 for additional insights into where Herod the tetrarch ruled. Also note who the high priest was.

Why is this incident important to the message of Matthew?

Now let's look at verses 13-21. Ask *who, what, when, where, why* and *how* about this event. What do you learn about Jesus and His disciples?

This event appears in all four Gospels. If you have the time and interest, read Mark 6:30-44, Luke 9:12-17, and John 6:5-15 to gain additional insights.

Now read Matthew 14:22-36 again, asking the 5 W's and an H about this event. What do you learn about faith, worship, and the Son?

What did the disciples see according to verses 15-21? What are they seeing *now?* What point is being driven home?

Do you believe these stories are true? How do they affect your faith? How do they affect sharing your faith?

Record a theme for Matthew 14 on MATTHEW AT A GLANCE.

DAY FOUR

Now read Matthew 15, marking the key words on your bookmark as well as time and geographical references. Add *tradition, Pharisees, heart,* and *defile.*

Read Matthew 15 again and mark the different events.

DAY FIVE

Now let's look at the event in verses 1-20. What are the traditions of the Pharisees? How does Jesus show that they're wrong?

What did you learn about the heart, and what application can you make? What about traditions? How do they affect your Christian walk? Are they more important to you than the Word of God?

How does Matthew 15:13-14 compare to Matthew 13:36-43?

If you have time, look up *Pharisees* and *traditions* in a Bible dictionary or encyclopedia.

DAY SIX

Look where you marked *faith* in Matthew 15:21-28. How does the Canaanite woman demonstrate her faith? Compare her faith to the faith mentioned in Hebrews 11:6. What do you see?

How does her faith contrast with the disciples' faith in Matthew 6:30 and 8:26?

Who has been Jesus' primary audience up to this point in Matthew? Where do most events happen? How does Matthew substantiate events in Jesus' life?

Now read verses 29-39. Where does this event occur, and who is there? Note differences between this event and the feeding of the 5000 in Matthew 14:13-21.

Now read Mark 7:31–8:20 and carefully observe the geographical references (the Decapolis was a Gentile region). Now read Romans 1:16. Any insights?

Don't forget to record a theme for Matthew 15 on MATTHEW AT A GLANCE.

DAY SEVEN

 Store in your heart: Matthew 15:18-19
Read and discuss: Matthew 14–15

QUESTIONS FOR DISCUSSION OR INDIVIDUAL STUDY

- ∾ Discuss the incident with Herod and John the Baptist. How do John's remarks to Herod compare with those he said in Matthew 3?

- ∾ Compare and contrast the feedings of the 5000 and the 4000.

- ∾ Discuss Jesus' walking on water. What did you learn about faith and worship?

- ∾ What did you learn about the Pharisees and scribes? How does it compare with what you already knew about them?

- ∾ What did you learn about the heart?

- ∾ What lessons can you draw from Jesus' encounter with the Canaanite woman?

THOUGHT FOR THE WEEK

In the tabernacle and in the temple, inside the holy place on the right was the table of showbread (the bread of the presence), reminding the Jews that God provided bread for them during their wilderness wandering. They were to remember to rely on Him always, trusting Him for food to live on.

According to chapter 6 of John's Gospel, after Jesus fed

the 5000 He said He was the bread of life. In the person of Jesus of Nazareth (the Messiah, the son of David and Abraham), God provided bread from heaven to bring eternal life. Those who come to Jesus will never hunger; those who believe in Him will never thirst.

What did Jesus do by feeding 5000 with only five loaves of bread? He proved that He could feed everyone. We know He could have fed more than 5000 because 12 baskets of food were left over.

Then He walked on water, showing His 12 disciples He had authority over creation. They were so skeptical, they thought He was a ghost, and even when He identified Himself and did what they asked, they still doubted. Yet they worshipped Him as God's Son. Their faith was "little." As Jews, they knew they were forbidden to worship anything but the one true God.

The Canaanite woman from the region of Tyre and Sidon (on the Mediterranean coast of modern-day Lebanon, north of Israel) worshipped Jesus even though He told her He was sent to Israel, not the nations. Her called *her* faith "great." Although He wasn't sent to the Gentiles, He acknowledged a Gentile with great faith. Her faith was similar to the centurion's (Matthew 8), whose faith Jesus said He had not seen anywhere in Israel.

Jesus followed this encounter with a believing Gentile by feeding 4000 with seven loaves and a few fish. Matthew says He did this along the Sea of Galilee; Mark's Gospel adds that it was in the region of the Decapolis. This area east of the Sea of Galilee was predominantly Gentile, as we can tell from the presence of the swine Jesus sent the demons into after He cast them out of the demoniacs.

So after Jesus' encounter with the Gentile Canaanite woman, He feeds 4000 Gentiles the same way He fed 5000 Jews. This reminds us that Jesus, the bread of life, came to feed Jews *and* Gentiles, and that Jews and Gentiles would come to Jesus in faith. Paul confirms this in Romans 1:16, where he says the gospel is the power for salvation, to the Jew first and then to the Greek. *Greek* is synonymous with *Gentile.*

So Matthew shows his Jewish audience that Jesus came to the Jews, but He also planned to save Gentiles, giving them the same bread of life He offered the Jews. That's great news for all of us who are Gentiles, isn't it?

Who Do You Say Jesus Is?

So who do *you* say Jesus is? The way you answer this question with both your mind and life will determine whether you live forever with Christ in heaven or spend eternity in hell. This is the single most important question you can answer.

DAY ONE

Today read Matthew 16, marking the key words from your bookmark. Also mark Jesus' titles in this chapter like *the Christ*. Don't forget references to time. You may want to note events in the margins of your Bible.

Record a theme for Matthew 16 on MATTHEW AT A GLANCE.

DAY TWO

The Pharisees and Sadducees separated over key doctrines but united to oppose Jesus and His message. In Matthew 16:1-12, who and what does Jesus warn about?

Read these verses to see what else you can learn about this group:

> Mark 7:3,5-8

> Luke 18:9-14

Mark *sign* in Matthew 16:1-12 and list what you learn. What is the sign of Jonah? What does Matthew 12:38-41 tell you about this sign?

List the questions and answers given in Matthew 16:13-20. Who has the right answer? How do you know?

Read Ephesians 2:19-22. How does this compare to what Jesus said in Matthew about building His church?

What do you learn about Jesus' future from Matthew 16:21-28?

DAY THREE

Read Matthew 17 today, marking the key words from your bookmark and geographical locations.

Record a theme for Matthew 17 on MATTHEW AT A GLANCE.

DAY FOUR

What happens in Matthew 17:1-8? Answer as many of the 5 W's and an H as you can.

What do you learn about Elijah in Matthew 17:9-13? Read Malachi 3:1-3; 4:5 and Matthew 11:11-14. How do these compare to Matthew 17:9-13?

What lessons do you learn from Matthew 17:14-27? List

the events in these verses and the main teaching principle from each.

DAY FIVE

Today's assignment is Matthew 18. Mark the key words from your bookmark, as well *woe, stumble,²* *stumbling block,³* and *forgive.⁴*

Record a theme for Matthew 18 on MATTHEW AT A GLANCE.

DAY SIX

What did you learn about children and stumbling in this chapter?

What is God's perspective on the lost from Matthew 18:10-14?

Matthew 18:15-20 is often quoted but often out of context. How should we approach a fellow Christian who is sinning?

Read Deuteronomy 19:15. What is the purpose for two or three witnesses?

What principles of forgiveness do we learn from Matthew 18?

DAY SEVEN

 Store in your heart: Matthew 16:15-16

Read and discuss: Matthew 16–18

QUESTIONS FOR DISCUSSION OR PERSONAL STUDY

- ❧ Discuss what you learned about the teachings of the Pharisees and Sadducees.

- ❧ Whom did people identify Jesus with? What is the truth about this, and why is it important? How does this fit into Matthew's purpose for writing his Gospel?

- ❧ What did Jesus tell His disciples about His future?

- ❧ Discuss the transfiguration. Who was there? What was the purpose? How does this event relate to Matthew 3? Who spoke? What was said?

- ❧ How do John the Baptist and Elijah relate?

- ❧ Discuss what you learned about faith from these chapters.

- ❧ Discuss children, stumbling, and believing.

- ❧ What did you learn about approaching a brother who sins? What are the steps? Why the order?

- ❧ Finally, what did you learn about forgiveness?

THOUGHT FOR THE WEEK

Matthew contains many truths, but three of the most widely known are the Great Commission, the Great Commandment, and the Great Confession. We'll see the first two in later chapters, but Matthew 16 contains the Great Confession. Jesus asked His disciples who people said He was, and the people's answers were wrong. But God granted Peter the understanding that Jesus was the Christ, the Son of the living God. This is the Great Confession: who Jesus really is.

Who do you say He is? Do you confess Him as the Messiah (Christ), the anointed one? Do you confess Him as the Son of the living God? The answer is crucial to your future. As Matthew's Gospel tells us, those who believe will enter the kingdom of heaven. Those who don't believe don't enter. What does that mean?

Jesus says He will build His church on the apostle Peter. Paul's letter to the Ephesians makes clear that Jesus is the cornerstone of the church and that the apostles and prophets are the foundation. Believers make up the rest of the building built on that foundation. Some take Peter's confession of Christ as the foundation Jesus builds on rather than Peter himself, and that's true because Jesus is the cornerstone. But it's also true that the church is built on Peter because he's *one of* the apostles in the foundation (so it's not built *exclusively* on him).

But what's important to you and me is that we're part of this building, the temple of the Holy Spirit. Each of us is a temple of the Holy Spirit, and collectively we're the temple of the Holy Spirit, the church.

What does this theological truth mean practically to our lives? First, it means that we need to consider how we live, what we do with our bodies. God commands us to be holy as He is holy. He tells us that if we join our bodies to a prostitute, we join Jesus to a prostitute and defile the temple. If we take seriously the idea that we are a temple of the Holy Spirit, we must take seriously how we live. If we take seriously our relationship to God, Jesus, and the Holy Spirit, we must take seriously what we do, how we live. Fornication not only demeans God's glory, it also defiles His temple.

Can we live perfectly? No, and so these chapters contain instructions on how to cleanse a defiled temple. First John 1:9 tells us that if we confess our sins, God will forgive us and cleanse us from all unrighteousness. But sometimes we don't voluntarily clean up our act. Sometimes we need help from someone who loves us.

In Matthew, one such help is called church discipline. How and why do we approach a sinning brother? The purpose is to cleanse him, restore him to holiness. This is why Jesus taught about forgiveness. When a brother repents, the church forgives him. He always remains a part of the building. He's always a temple of the Holy Spirit, though he'll need cleaning up until the day of the Lord Jesus (Philippians 1:6).

And as we help him clean up, we need to remember what Jesus said in Matthew 7 about taking the log out of our own eye before removing the speck in our brother's. We can't see to take a speck out if we've got a log in our eye. We must hold ourselves to the same standard we hold others to because we're judged by the same standard.

So, what do *you* believe about Jesus? Who is He? What is your relationship to Him? Do you need to do some "house cleaning"? Can you help someone else clean up? Do you forgive others?

The Last Shall Be First, and the First Shall Be Last

First, last, greatest, least. Jesus came to serve *all*. Does He expect the same from His followers?

DAY ONE

We're going to tackle two chapters again this week. Today read Matthew 19 and mark the key words from your bookmark. In verses 1-12 mark *divorce*,[5] but don't add it to your bookmark.

Determine a theme for Matthew 19 and add it to MATTHEW AT A GLANCE.

DAY TWO

What did you learn about divorce in Matthew 19:1-12?

Read 1 Corinthians 6:12–7:9 and Ephesians 5:22-25,33. How do these verses add to your understanding of God's plan for marriage? Are there good reasons *not* to marry?

According to verses 13-15, children teach us a valuable lesson about the kingdom of heaven. How does this lesson compare to what you learned last week in Matthew 18?

DAYS THREE & FOUR

Let's look at Matthew 19:16-26. You might want to underline or mark references to the rich young man.

Read these verses. How do they relate to the young man's question?

Leviticus 18:1-5

Deuteronomy 28:1-2,13-15

Deuteronomy 30:19-20

Deuteronomy 32:45-47

How do these verses relate to Jesus' answer?

Matthew 6:19-21

Matthew 6:24

Matthew 6:31-33

Matthew 10:38-39

Matthew 16:24-26

DAY FIVE

Today we'll move on to Matthew 20, where Jesus uses another parable to describe the kingdom of heaven. Read the chapter and mark the key words and phrases. Mark *landowner,*[6] but don't add it to your bookmark. Don't forget to mark time and geographical references.

Record a theme for Matthew 20 on MATTHEW AT A GLANCE.

DAY SIX

What is the main point of the parable of the land-owner?

How do you understand the landowner paying the same amount to the first and last hired? What do you learn from the response of the first hired?

Are any other points in this parable consistent with Matthew's emphases?

After Jesus teaches this parable, where is He? What does He say to His disciples, and what does the mother of Zebedee ask for? How does her request tie into the principle of the parable?

When Jesus asks His disciples if they can drink His cup, they say they can, and He says they will. What cup is He referring to?

Read John 13:3-4,12-17. This familiar story is not found in Matthew. How does it relate to the teaching we've just read in Matthew 20?

DAY SEVEN

 Store in your heart: Matthew 20:28

Read and discuss: Matthew 19–20

QUESTIONS FOR DISCUSSION OR PERSONAL STUDY

ᴄᴠ Discuss what you learned about marriage and divorce. Keep the discussion focused on God's Word.

∞ What did you learn about the kingdom of heaven from the example of children?

∞ Discuss what you learned from the young man who asked how to obtain eternal life.

∞ What does "the last shall be first, and the first last" mean?

∞ Discuss the parable of the landowner. Who do the characters represent? What principles are taught here?

∞ What characteristics of Jesus do you learn about in these chapters?

∞ What's the connection between greatness and service?

THOUGHT FOR THE WEEK

I've taken many tour groups to Israel over the years, teaching the Bible in the land of the Bible. One thing I've noticed about Jews, Arabs (Muslim *and* Christian), and tourists from all over the world is that they need to be first.

I've also been to other countries where pushing to the front seems to be a way of life. Getting on airplanes, entering subways and trains, moving through the marketplace, driving on congested streets...people seem to have the common behavior of pushing to be first. Sadly, I've even seen it in crowds peering into the empty Garden Tomb in Jerusalem.

It just doesn't seem natural for people to form a line and wait their turn. That appears to be a trait peculiar to only a few cultures. Letting others go first was certainly Jesus' idea, straight from this part of Matthew.

Polite behavior is rare and usually absent in countries

with non-Christian heritages...which begs this question: Where did the idea of letting others go first originate?

Watch society around you, and you'll see that politeness was certainly not handed down from a fallen Adam. Patience, love, and self-control are all part of the fruit of the Spirit. So is thinking more highly of others than yourself, as Paul taught in his letter to the Philippians. But even Paul didn't invent this idea; he summed it up as the mind as Christ.

Jesus taught servanthood instead of "win, place, or show." "Servant leadership" is a popular phrase today. It reflects the Golden Rule. Treat others the way you want to be treated. Give them a chance; be polite. Think about them before yourself. If you lead others, lead in a way that builds them up and enables them to accomplish God's purposes in their lives. Serve them while leading.

When you put others before yourself, you'll be surprised how some people mock you and tell you you're a sucker, a fool, and that you'll never get ahead in this world. And they could be right. Just remember what it will do for you in the kingdom of heaven.

This is part of Jesus' radical message of a kingdom that is not of this world. God's heavenly kingdom brings to earth a completely different set of values. The ruler of this world—the prince of the power of the air and of the powers of darkness, the accuser of the brethren, the father of all lies—would have us say, "Me first!" That's how he tempted Jesus in Matthew 4. "Think about yourself; look what you can have"—that's what he seemed to be saying. But Jesus resisted, becoming an example to us. Think about the kingdom of heaven. Act as if your citizenship is in heaven, because it is. Act like you're an alien and stranger on this earth, because you are.

> Do nothing from selfishness or empty conceit,
> but with humility of mind regard one another

as more important than yourselves; do not merely look out for your own personal interests, but also for the interests of others. Have this attitude in yourselves which was also in Christ Jesus, who, although He existed in the form of God, did not regard equality with God a thing to be grasped, but emptied Himself, taking the form of a bond-servant, and being made in the likeness of men. Being found in appearance as a man, He humbled Himself by becoming obedient to the point of death, even death on a cross (Philippians 2:3-8).

BLESSED IS HE WHO COMES IN THE NAME OF THE LORD

The King is coming! Not on a white horse, but on a donkey! What kind of Messiah is this? How can someone on a donkey throw off the oppression of the Romans? Yet the crowds praised Jesus. They shouted, "Hosanna!"

DAY ONE

This week we'll cover three chapters. Read Matthew 21, mark key words and phrases, and ask the 5 W's and an H questions to learn what the chapter is about. Slow down and focus on the message; it's not just about marking.

Have you ever thought about how awesome it is to be able to spend time in the Word of God? For centuries, Bible study was only for an elite few, but now we can sit in our homes or offices and study for ourselves.

Record a theme for Matthew 21 on MATTHEW AT A GLANCE.

DAY TWO

Matthew 21:1-9 describes the triumphal entry. People spread palm branches on the road (John 12:12-13), and

91

it was the first day of the week, so the day is called Palm Sunday.

Note how this event fulfilled Scripture. Also note what the people called Jesus. This chapter includes other events, so note each one and what you learn. Especially watch people's reactions to what Jesus says and does in each event.

There are two more parables in this chapter. Read and note the main point of each. Again note whom Jesus is addressing these parables to and how people react to what He says.

DAY THREE

Read Matthew 22, marking key words as usual.

Record a theme for Matthew 22 on MATTHEW AT A GLANCE.

DAY FOUR

Jesus speaks parables to the Pharisees again. What is the parable in Matthew 22:1-14 about?

Wedding customs in Jesus' day are keys to understanding some of His teachings. Read these verses for more insight:

Matthew 9:14-18

John 3:25-30

Revelation 19:1-8

Whom do the characters in this parable represent? See how the Pharisees react in verse 15. Did they understand the parable?

How did the Pharisees and Sadducees try to trap Jesus in the rest of Matthew 22? Note the main points in each encounter.

How does Jesus trap the Pharisees in verses 41-46? What point is He making about Himself?

DAY FIVE

For our last chapter of the week, read Matthew 23, marking key words and phrases from your bookmark. Also mark *hypocrites* and *swears,* but don't add them to the bookmark.

Record a theme for Matthew 23 on *MATTHEW AT A GLANCE.*

DAY SIX

List what you learned about the Pharisees and scribes. How are they hypocrites? Fit their traits to modern times— are there hypocrites today?

What are the two greatest commandments? Read Deuteronomy 6:4-9,17-25. How can we obey these commands today?

Finally, read 1 John 4:7-12,19-21. What do you learn about love?

DAY SEVEN

 Store in your heart: Matthew 22:37-39

Read and discuss: Matthew 21–23

QUESTIONS FOR DISCUSSION OR PERSONAL STUDY

∾ Discuss insights you received from the parables in Matthew 21. How did they reveal the chief priests' and Pharisees' errors?

∾ Discuss the parable of the wedding feast in Matthew 22. What errors does it reveal?

∾ What did John the Baptist call the Pharisees and Sadducees to do? How did the chief priests and Pharisees respond to Jesus' parables? What do you learn about them?

∾ Review the ways the Pharisees and Sadducees tried to trap Jesus.

∾ Was Jesus right to call the Pharisees and scribes hypocrites? How so?

THOUGHT FOR THE WEEK

As Jesus approached Jerusalem from Bethphage on the Mount of Olives, the multitude that had followed Him from Jericho threw their garments on the road, cut branches from trees, and spread them on the road. And they cried out, "Hosanna to the Son of David; blessed is He who comes in the name of the Lord; hosanna in the highest!"

But the city of Jerusalem was stirred up, asking, "Who is this?" After all, this Jesus of Nazareth came riding into the city on a donkey, and these people were acclaiming Him as the Son of David. Expectations among Jews of the day were a bit higher for the Son of David, the Messiah. They expected a conquering hero riding a horse, coming to rescue them from the oppression of the Romans. So who was this, riding a donkey?

First of all, He was fulfilling prophecy. Matthew 21:4 tells us that this fulfilled prophecy, and comparing texts, the quote is from Zechariah 9:9. But why a donkey?

When coming to a city, kings could indicate their intent by what they rode. If their intent was peace, they rode a donkey. If their intent was to conquer, they rode a horse. Compare Jesus' entry to Jerusalem in Matthew to His return to earth in Revelation 19:11-16. Isaiah presented the child to be born as the Prince of Peace and explained that there would be no end to the increase of His government or of peace.

When Jesus read from Isaiah 61 in the synagogue in Nazareth (Luke 4), He stopped after reading that He was to proclaim the favorable year of the Lord, and He said that the scripture had been fulfilled in their hearing. He did not continue because the next line prophesied the day of vengeance of our God. His first coming was to bring good news to the afflicted, to bind up the brokenhearted, and to proclaim liberty to captives and freedom to prisoners. At His second coming, He will usher in the day of vengeance. That's why in Revelation 19, Jesus comes on a white horse. That's when He comes to conquer and make war against the enemies of God.

Luke also tells us that at Jesus' birth, the heavenly host praised God, saying, "On earth peace among men with whom He is pleased." His first coming, His incarnation as Immanuel, God with us, was to establish peace.

That's what Ephesians 2:14-15 tells us: Jesus is our peace, and in His crucifixion, He abolished the enmity, the Law, preaching peace to those who were near and those who were far off. Romans 5 tells us the same, that having been justified by faith, we have peace with God.

In all of Paul's letters, in Hebrews, and in Peter's letters, the wish for the reader is peace. God brings peace to those who receive Jesus as God the Son, those who believe the good news.

But for those who reject Jesus, there is no peace. Jesus will return on the day of vengeance of God with a sharp sword to strike the nations, and He will tread the winepress of the fierce wrath of God. On that day, He will ride a white horse, and the host with Him will ride white horses.

Those with Jesus at His triumphal entry into Jerusalem cried, "Hosanna!" which can be translated, "Save us!" This word originally was a prayer addressed to God, meaning "O save us now" (see Psalm 118:25). Later it came to be used as a shout of praise (like "Hallelujah!") and then as an enthusiastic welcome to pilgrims or to a famous rabbi. "Hosanna in the highest" likely means, "Save us, O God, who lives in heaven." Its use by the multitudes with Jesus may well reflect a mixture of all these elements, depending on the view of the one shouting. The reality is that He was named Jesus because He would save the people from their sins. For those who believed, He did.

There are no shouts of acclamation recorded in Revelation at Jesus' second coming. His return is for vengeance and wrath. In those days, men will hide in fear as they recognize the wrath of God coming upon those who do not believe. There will be no palm branches, no coats thrown on the road welcoming Jesus. The nations will war against Him but will be defeated. Then He will rule with a rod of iron. And those who are defeated will be thrown into the lake of fire, which burns eternally.

Until that day comes, though, there is time to escape. There is time for the gospel to be preached and for people to hear and believe. The call we have is to share in this peace-making effort by sharing the good news. Will you?

WHAT WILL BE THE SIGN OF HIS COMING?

~~~~~~

In the parable of the wheat and tares in chapter 13, Jesus speaks of the judgment at the end of the age. In chapter 16, He says He's coming with His angels to repay every man according to his deeds. Now in chapter 24, the disciples want to know how they'll know *when* He's coming.

DAY ONE

Read Matthew 24–25 to get the flow of thought. What are these two chapters about?

Now read Matthew 24 again and mark the key words and phrases from your bookmark. Also mark *temple (house)*, *tribulation,*[7] *nations, elect, be on the alert, be ready,* and references to the coming of the Son of Man, including time references.

Record a theme for Matthew 24 on MATTHEW AT A GLANCE.

DAY TWO

Read Matthew 23:37–24:3. What festival is at hand, and what are the chief priests and elders planning?

What "house" will be left desolate?

What did you learn from the words you marked? How does "the end" relate to previous teachings in Matthew? If you've forgotten, review Matthew 10:22-23 and Matthew 13:39-40,49.

What is the exhortation to those hearing this message?

Compare Revelation 14:6-7 with Matthew 24:14. What do you learn about God?

DAY THREE

What is the abomination of desolation Daniel spoke about? (Read Daniel 12:9-11, Daniel 9:27, and 2 Thessalonians 2:1-4.) Is there a temple at this time? Who receives this tribulation? Read Jeremiah 30:5-7.

From Matthew 24, what events precede the coming of the Son of Man?

According to Matthew 24:42-51, what happens when He comes? How does this compare to what you've seen in Matthew 13 and other places in Matthew?

DAY FOUR

Read Matthew 25, marking the key words on your bookmark.

Record a theme for Matthew 25 on MATTHEW AT A GLANCE.

DAY FIVE

Jesus compares the kingdom of heaven to several things in Matthew 25. We'll work our way through each. Remember that they relate to the coming of the Son of Man at the end of the age.

What happened to the five foolish virgins unprepared for the bridegroom? From your study of Matthew so far, who do you think the bridegroom represents?

What do you learn from the parable of the talents? Who is the master? Who are the slaves?

DAY SIX

Who do the sheep and the goats represent? How do they relate to the wheat and tares and to the good and bad fish in Matthew 13?

Let's look at the phrase "weeping and gnashing of teeth." Read these verses in Matthew: 8:12; 13:42,50; 22:13; 24:41; 25:30. What do we learn about those who do this and the place they go?

Who are Jesus' brothers (25:40)? How do you know?

DAY SEVEN

Store in your heart: Matthew 25:31
Read and discuss: Matthew 24–25

QUESTIONS FOR DISCUSSION OR PERSONAL STUDY

- ∾ Discuss the disciples' questions and Jesus' answers.

- ∾ What is the relationship between "the end" and the coming of the Son of Man?

- ∾ Review events leading up to the end.

- ∾ Discuss the relationship between the great tribulation and the abomination of desolation.

- ∾ What events occur at the coming of the Son of Man? How do these relate to the parables in Matthew 13?

- ∾ What are the exhortations to the disciples about the coming of the Son of Man?

- ∾ Discuss the parables of the ten virgins and the talents. What are the lessons from each?

- ∾ Discuss the judgment of the sheep and goats.

- ∾ What lesson is there for us in this judgment? Who are Jesus' brothers?

THOUGHT FOR THE WEEK

The biggest type in newspapers is reserved for the headlines of the biggest story. Interestingly, in the printing trade, the largest type used to be called *Second Coming*. Why? Among journalists decades ago, the biggest story they could think of was the second coming of the Lord. Whether the typesetters were being cynical, we'll never know. The type has been used for war, death of presidents, and other great news, but as one wag put it, "Only the journalists would be left behind to run that story."

The generation just prior to Jesus' return described in

Matthew 24 is like the one in the days of Noah—eating, drinking, marrying, doing all kinds of normal activities. Life was routine…at least until Noah arrived and preached "Repent!" for a hundred years. Then he built an ark and loaded it with living creatures, but no one repented. When the rains came, they were swept away by the flood—judgment for their sin.

The second coming will be like this. People will be living their lives, doing routine things, but not looking for His coming. That's what makes the disciples different. They ask Jesus for signs so they can look for His return. They want to be prepared. They plan to obey Jesus' exhortations to be ready, to be on the alert. They understand judgment will occur.

What do these exhortations mean for us? People alive at Jesus' return face judgment; the unrighteous will face eternal punishment. What do we do? Can we help them?

The answer is yes! Those who know what the future holds have the key to Hades and death: the gospel. Remember what Matthew 24:14 says: "This gospel of the kingdom shall be preached in the whole world as a testimony to all the nations, and then the end will come."

The only way anyone can avoid the judgment of "outer darkness, where there is weeping and gnashing of teeth" is by believing the gospel. But people can't believe something they haven't heard. And that's where you and I come in—sharing the gospel.

Romans 10 explicitly says that those who haven't heard the gospel can't believe it, and they can't hear it unless there's a preacher, and there isn't a preacher unless someone is sent. You can share (preach) the gospel or send a preacher; either way the gospel is shared. Now, Romans 10 is about the Jewish people. In fact, Romans 10–12 is about the gospel and the Jews. But preaching the gospel applies to all the lost,

Jew and Gentile alike. At Christ's coming, all who haven't believed will face the judgment of eternal punishment.

Now *you* have the truth. You've studied Matthew, so you know the gospel. All you have to do is share it. Not everyone will believe, but that's not your responsibility or your fault. Your duty is sharing. Try it! Remember, you're commanded to love your neighbors as yourself, and what better expression of love is there than to reach out to them with the saving truth of the gospel!

MAKE DISCIPLES

∾∾∾∾

Three years of ministry, healings, teachings, parables. Now, finally, we come to Jesus' death, burial, and resurrection. These events are not the end because He's coming back. But they are the last events recorded in Matthew's Gospel except for one significant final instruction Jesus gives His disciples.

DAY ONE

Read Matthew 26, marking key words and phrases from your bookmark as usual. Also mark *Passover, blood, crucifixion (crucified), raised (risen), covenant,* and *betray.*[8]

Record a theme for Matthew 26 on MATTHEW AT A GLANCE.

DAY TWO

This is a long chapter with many important topics, but they're straightforward and easy to understand. Let's take them one at a time, reaching for the main point instead of getting bogged down in details.

What is the setting at the start of the chapter? What major event awaits Jesus?

Now let's relate other people's actions to Jesus' crucifixion: What did the woman with perfume do? What did Judas do?

What is the significance of the supper Jesus and His disciples shared? How does it relate to Passover and to the crucifixion? Read Jeremiah 31:31-34 and 1 Corinthians 11:23-26.

What do you learn from Jesus and His disciples in the Garden of Gethsemane that you can apply to your life?

When Jesus is before Caiaphas, what is He accused of? What do the people want to know, and why? On what basis do they think He should die?

Finally, what do you learn from Peter's actions in the Garden of Gethsemane and at Caiaphas' house?

DAY THREE

Read through Matthew 27 before marking. When you go back to mark, make sure to catch the phrase *Son of God*.

Record a theme for Matthew 27 on MATTHEW AT A GLANCE.

DAYS FOUR & FIVE

What happens to Judas in Matthew 27?

Who are the main characters in Jesus' trial before Pilate? What does each want? Does the text tell you why they think they're doing the right thing?

When Jesus is scourged and then crucified, what do people say about Him? How do these opinions relate to the title "Son of God" Matthew highlights? Review what Satan said to Jesus in Matthew 4 and compare it to anything similar in Matthew 27.

The details of Jesus' trials, scourging, and crucifixion are staggeringly brutal and hard to believe even if you've seen movies like *The Passion of the Christ*. Read the following prophesies of events fulfilled in Matthew 27. They'll give you a greater appreciation for God's predetermined plan (Acts 2:23) to give His Son for us:

> Isaiah 50:6-7
>
> Isaiah 52:13–53:12
>
> Psalm 22:1-18

Matthew says Jesus cried out with a loud voice before He died. John 19:30 tells us He spoke a Greek word that was used to declare the full payment of a debt. Lenders would write *tetelestai*—"it is complete"—on a certificate of debt and then nail it up in a prominent place for all to see. If the debt were a mortgage, the certificate was nailed to the doorpost of the house.

What was nailed in Jesus' case, and where? Read Colossians 2:13-14. When Jesus gave up His spirit, the veil in the temple was torn in two. Read Hebrews 10:19-20. What do we have now because of Jesus' crucifixion?

DAY SIX

Our final chapter on this last day of study is Matthew 28. Read and mark Matthew 28. Mark *risen*.

Chapter 28 completes the Gospel according to Matthew in two ways: It's the last chapter, and it presents the climactic victory—the resurrection.

Read 1 Corinthians 15:1-8. What are the two elements of the gospel "according to the Scriptures"? How does Jesus' burial relate to His death? How did the witnesses relate to His resurrection?

Who witnessed Jesus' resurrection, according to Matthew 28?

Finally, what does Jesus command in Matthew 28:19-20? The main verb phrase is "make disciples." Some translate the Greek verb *poreuthentes* as a perfect (indicative) participle, "having gone," instead of most versions' imperative, "Go!" "Baptizing" and "teaching" are present participles, describing ongoing actions that define "make disciples."

Now, where did Jesus command His disciples to go, what are they to do, and for how long?

How important is this command to you? How does it challenge you?

Finally, record a theme for Matthew 28 on *MATTHEW AT A GLANCE*.

DAY SEVEN

 Store in your heart: Matthew 28:19-20
Read and discuss: Matthew 26–28

QUESTIONS FOR DISCUSSION OR PERSONAL STUDY

∽ To set the stage for more in-depth topical discussion of these chapters, start by reviewing events from the Passover meal to Jesus' command to make disciples.

෴ Discuss the significance of the Passover supper Jesus ate with His disciples.

෴ What did you learn about Judas in these chapters?

෴ What did you learn from events in the Garden of Gethsemane before Jesus' arrest?

෴ Discuss Jesus' arrest and trial before Caiaphas. Don't miss the accusations.

෴ Peter is an interesting character in these events. What did you learn from him?

෴ Discuss Pilate's trial of Jesus. Who were Jesus' accusers?

෴ What significance did you find in the details of Jesus' death? Remember to compare Matthew to the cross-references in Isaiah and Psalms.

෴ Why is Jesus' resurrection important?

෴ Finally, what is your reaction to Jesus' command in the last two verses of Matthew? What application will you make in your life?

THOUGHT FOR THE WEEK

The death, burial, and resurrection of Jesus Christ are the most important historical events in the history of mankind since the fall of man in the garden of Eden. Why?

When Adam and Eve sinned, God shed the blood of an animal to make coverings for their nakedness. Then He told them a seed from Eve would crush the serpent's head, although the serpent would bruise His heel.

The serpent was Satan. The seed was Jesus. Abraham was promised the same seed, and he believed and was declared righteous. God later shed the blood of His only begotten Son to atone for man's sin. The Law, with all its feasts, sacrifices, and other worship rituals, was a schoolmaster that led us to Christ.

So we see that Christ the Passover Lamb was slain. The book of Hebrews says there is no forgiveness of sins without the shedding of blood. It adds that the blood of bulls and goats is not enough. It takes the sinless Christ, born of a virgin (so Adam's sin is not passed along), to shed sinless blood. He who knew no sin was made sin for us—the sin of all mankind was placed on Him. His blood alone atones for mankind's sin. And although the sacrifices under the Law were made year after year, Hebrews tells us that Jesus died once for all: one Lamb, one sacrifice.

The veil in the temple was torn in two from top to bottom when Christ died, a sure indication that God did the tearing. Jewish historian Josephus wrote that it would take two teams of oxen pulling in opposite directions to tear it in two. And the veil, Hebrews tells us, was the flesh of Christ. The veil represented the barrier that separated man from God. Beyond the veil was the holy of holies, where the ark and the mercy seat that covered the ark were (in the tabernacle and Solomon's temple), and where God met with Israel. Only the high priest could enter—once a year, and with blood. If he wasn't properly cleansed, he died.

Because of sin, mankind cannot approach God. The wages of sin is death. Sin must be atoned for. Man must be cleansed, washed in the blood of a spotless, sinless Lamb. Christ provided that sinless blood through His torn flesh. We are cleansed, and we have access to God. We can come boldly to the throne of grace. The sacrifice of Christ gives us the cleansing we need.

But the death of Christ is not all there is to the gospel. The cross is empty, and Jesus was buried, proving that He truly died. The grave is also empty. His body wasn't stolen as the Jews and Romans claimed. He rose from the dead and was seen by many witnesses, some still alive in Paul's time. That's the other main point of the gospel—the resurrection. We have not only access to God and forgiveness of sins but also life, just as Jesus has life. Beyond this earthly life, we have life for all eternity.

All who believe the gospel will have that eternal life in spite of tribulation, persecution, or other terrible things that happen in this life. That's the promise, and it's guaranteed by God!

What does God want us to do in response to His gracious gift? Make disciples in all the nations, baptize them, and teach them to obey all Jesus commanded. He promises to be with us to the end of the age. We don't know when Jesus is coming back, but He's with us in the Holy Spirit until then. That's good news, isn't it? That's what *gospel* means— good news. Matthew the tax collector, one of the 12 disciples of Christ, gave us this good news of Jesus Christ: His death, burial, and resurrection, and the guarantee of eternal life for all those who believe in all the nations. That's you and me. Rejoice!

APPENDIX

Theme of Matthew:

SEGMENT DIVISIONS

Author:

Date:

Purpose:

Key Words:

king (kingdom,
kingdom of
heaven, kingdom
of God)

fulfilled

the devil or
demons

covenant

Spirit (Holy Spirit)

believe (faith)

disciples
(disciple)

sign (signs)

		CHAPTER THEMES
		1 Jesus is man AND son of God
		2
		3
		4
		5
		6
		7
		8
		9
		10
		11
		12
		13
		14
		15
		16
		17
		18
		19
		20
		21
		22
		23
		24
		25
		26
		27
		28

BIBLE CITIES IN THE TIME OF JESUS

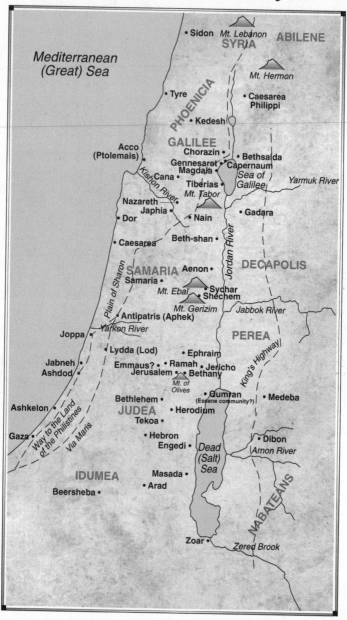

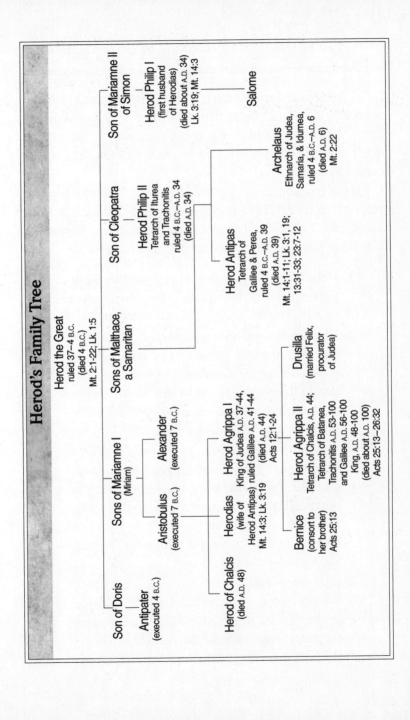

Herod's Family Tree

Herod the Great
ruled 37–4 B.C.
(died 4 B.C.)
Mt. 2:1-22; Lk. 1:5

Son of Doris

Antipater
(executed 4 B.C.)

Sons of Mariamne I
(Miriam)

Alexander
(executed 7 B.C.)

Aristobulus
(executed 7 B.C.)

Herod Agrippa I
King of Judea A.D. 37-44,
ruled Galilee A.D. 41-44
(died A.D. 44)
Acts 12:1-24

Herodias
(wife of
Herod Antipas)
Mt. 14:3; Lk. 3:19

Herod of Chalcis
(died A.D. 48)

Herod Agrippa II
Tetrarch of Chalcis, A.D. 44;
Tetrarch of Batanea,
Trachonitis A.D. 53-100
and Galilee A.D. 56-100
King, A.D. 48-100
(died about A.D. 100)
Acts 25:13—26:32

Bernice
(consort to
her brother)
Acts 25:13

Drusilla
(married Felix,
procurator
of Judea)

**Sons of Malthace,
a Samaritan**

Herod Antipas
Tetrarch of
Galilee & Perea,
ruled 4 B.C.–A.D. 39
(died A.D. 39)
Mt. 14:1-11; Lk. 3:1, 19;
13:31-33; 23:7-12

Archelaus
Ethnarch of Judea,
Samaria, & Idumea,
ruled 4 B.C.–A.D. 6
(died A.D. 6)
Mt. 2:22

Son of Cleopatra

Herod Philip II
Tetrarch of Iturea
and Trachonitis
ruled 4 B.C.–A.D. 34
(died A.D. 34)

**Son of Mariamne II
of Simon**

Herod Philip I
(first husband
of Herodias)
(died about A.D. 34)
Lk. 3:19; Mt. 14:3

Salome

INTERPRETING AND UNDERSTANDING PARABLES

A parable is a story which, although not usually factual, is true to life, teaching a universal moral lesson or truth. Every detail of a parable reinforces the main theme, so you don't have to ascribe a specific spiritual meaning and application to each point.

Jesus frequently used parables in His teaching for two reasons: to reveal truth to believers and to hide truth from those who rejected it because their hearts were hardened. Use these steps to properly interpret a parable:

1. Determine the occasion of the parable. Since parables clarify or emphasize a truth, discover why the parable was told. What prompted it?

2. Look for the intended meaning of the parable. The meaning will sometimes be stated. If not, it usually can be determined by the application of the parable to the hearer. Don't impose any meaning beyond what the speaker clearly stated or applied to the hearers.

3. Identify the central idea of the parable. Every parable has a central theme or emphasis. Don't give details of the story meaning if they're independent of the main teaching of the parable, but identify relevant details. Again, a detail is relevant only if it reinforces the central theme of the parable.

4. Interpret parables in the context of the culture of Bible times, not today's culture. For example, in the parable of the wise and foolish virgins, the central emphasis of the parable is, "Be on the alert then, for you do not know the day nor

the hour" (Matthew 25:13). Understanding Eastern wedding traditions gives insight into the parable and explains why some were ready and others were not.

5. Do not establish doctrine when parables are the primary or only source for that teaching. Parables should amplify or affirm doctrine, not establish it.

Notes

1. KJV: take thought
2. KJV: offend; NKJV, NIV, ESV: sin
3. KJV, NKJV: offense; ESV: temptation
4. NIV: cancelled
5. KJV: put away
6. KJV: householder; ESV: master of a house
7. NIV: distress
8. KJV, NKJV, ESV: deliver; NIV: hand him over

NOTES FOR PERSONAL STUDY

Notes for Personal Study

NOTES FOR PERSONAL STUDY

NOTES FOR PERSONAL STUDY

Notes for Personal Study

NOTES FOR PERSONAL STUDY

NOTES FOR PERSONAL STUDY

BOOKS IN THE
NEW INDUCTIVE STUDY SERIES

ᘏᘏᘏᘏ

Teach Me Your Ways
Genesis, Exodus,
Leviticus, Numbers, Deuteronomy

*Choosing Victory,
Overcoming Defeat*
Joshua, Judges, Ruth

Desiring God's Own Heart
1 & 2 Samuel, 1 Chronicles

Walking Faithfully with God
1 & 2 Kings, 2 Chronicles

*Overcoming Fear
and Discouragement*
Ezra, Nehemiah, Esther

*Trusting God
in Times of Adversity*
Job

*Praising God Through
Prayer and Worship*
Psalms

*God's Answers for
Today's Problems*
Proverbs

Face-to-Face with a Holy God
Isaiah

*God's Blueprint
for Bible Prophecy*
Daniel

*Discovering the God
of Second Chances*
Jonah, Joel, Amos, Obadiah

*Finding Hope
When Life Seems Dark*
Hosea, Micah, Nahum,
Habakkuk, Zephaniah

*Opening the Windows
of Blessing*
Haggai, Zechariah, Malachi

The Coming of God's Kingdom
Matthew

The Call to Follow Jesus
Luke

*The God Who Cares
and Knows You*
John

*The Holy Spirit
Unleashed in You*
Acts

*God's Answers for
Relationships and Passions*
1 & 2 Corinthians

*Free from Bondage
God's Way*
Galatians, Ephesians

That I May Know Him
Philippians, Colossians

*Standing Firm in
These Last Days*
1 & 2 Thessalonians

*Walking in Power,
Love, and Discipline*
1 & 2 Timothy, Titus

*Living with Discernment
in the End Times*
1 & 2 Peter, Jude

God's Love Alive in You
1, 2, & 3 John,
Philemon, James

Behold, Jesus Is Coming!
Revelation

NEW AMERICAN STANDARD BIBLE
UPDATED EDITION

THE NEW INDUCTIVE STUDY BIBLE

DISCOVERING THE TRUTH FOR YOURSELF

CHANGING THE WAY PEOPLE STUDY GOD'S WORD

"Inductive study of the Bible is the best way to discover scriptural truth...There is no jewel more precious than that which you have mined yourself."

—HOWARD HENDRICKS

Every feature is designed to help you gain a more intimate understanding of God and His Word. This study Bible, the only one based entirely on the inductive study approach, provides you with the tools for observing what the text says, interpreting what it means, and applying it to your life.

☐ **YES!** I am interested in receiving a free gift to help me in my inductive Bible study.

☐ I am interested in information that will direct me to an inductive Bible study group in my area.

☐ I am interested in further training on how to study my Bible inductively. Please send me information on how to know God and His Word in a more personal way.

☐ I am interested in information about inductive Bible study for my church.

Name _____

Address _____

City _____ State _____ ZIP _____

Daytime Phone (_____) _____ Email _____

Precept Ministries exists for the sole purpose of establishing people in God's Word. We desire to help you minister more effectively to others.